W9-CEW-646

By His Mercy 2: Living All In
How 13 Ordinary Catholics have seen
God's Extraordinary Mercy

By His Mercy 2: Living All In

How 13 Ordinary Catholics have seen
God's Extraordinary Mercy

Tricia Walz

Sophie Cash
Kate Shermach
Lucas Gerads
Theresa Lieser
James Uthmeier
Mary Solarz
Sarah Dvoracek
Ryan Myklebust
Lisa Cash
Heather Pfannenstein
Ben Owen-Block
Sr. Anne Thérèse Wilder, O.P.
Colette Jemming

Cover by Rachel Warner

Tricia Walz
2019

Copyright © 2019 by Tricia Walz

All rights reserved. This book or any portion thereof may not be reproduced or used in any manner whatsoever without the express written permission of the publisher except for the use of brief quotations in a book review or scholarly journal.

First Printing: 2019

ISBN 978-0-359-82337-6

Tricia Walz
Saint Cloud, MN 56303

Cover Artist: Rachel Warner

Contents

Acknowledgements

We have so many incredible people to thank! First of all, we would like to thank all of our priests and religious who so willingly give their lives to serve the Lord. Thank you so much for your powerful witness and your daily sacrifices for the Church!

We would also like to thank our family and friends who have supported and encouraged us throughout the years and throughout the publication of this book.

A special thanks to Nikki Silbernick, Ann Marschel, Sally Traut, Kim Walz and Briana Alba for their help editing our testimonies, and to Mark McGowan for all his help with formatting.

Finally, above all, we would like to thank the Lord for showing us His loving mercy and for this opportunity to share our testimonies with you!

Foreword

After the incredibly overwhelming response from our first *By His Mercy* book, I realized just how much we thirst for concrete stories of God's mercy and love. As Catholics, I do not think we share our experiences as quickly and openly as we should, and I have come to understand just how important and necessary it is to share the ways that God has revealed Himself in our lives, whether in big or small ways.

Sharing your testimony first of all requires vulnerability. It is hard to admit our struggles and imperfections to people we do know, much less to people we have never met. It also requires surrender, recognizing that we do not have control over our lives and allowing God, the author of our stories, to use those stories as He wishes. It is truly amazing how God can use our stories to help shape others' stories.

When I was praying about this book, a certain phrase wouldn't leave my mind: *Living all in.* This is the mission of each of us. One of the hardest things in life is to trust in the Lord and to surrender to His Will. Living all in is being completely abandoned to God in everything. The paradox of Christianity is that the more we give our lives away, the more joy we receive in return! St. Thérèse of Lisieux once said, "You cannot be half a saint. You must be a whole saint or no saint at all." The world thinks that freedom comes from clinging to our lives and grasping at worldly ideals, but Jesus teaches us that real freedom comes from giving our life away, abandoning ourselves entirely to His will.

As I read and re-read the testimonies in this book, I am struck by just how different "living all in" looks for each person, but how they are each following the mission He has given them. I sincerely hope you are uplifted by this book and I am truly humbled to have been able to be a part of it!

*Jesus does not demand great actions from us
but simply surrender and gratitude.*
-St. Thérèse of Lisieux

Tricia Walz
August 2019

Sophie Cash

"It is Jesus that you seek when you dream of happiness; He is waiting for you when nothing else you find satisfies you; He is the beauty to which you are so attracted; it is He who provoked you with that thirst for fullness that will not let you settle for compromise; it is He who urges you to shed the masks of a false life; it is He who reads in your hearts your most genuine choices, the choices that others try to stifle."

-Pope St. John Paul II

I accidentally read the first *By His Mercy* book in one sitting. I was captivated. Reading the stories of people that I actually *knew* and the miracles they experienced blew me away. (I'm not going to lie, I actually fangirled a few times.) But, when I put the book down, I looked over to my younger brother (who had already read the book) and simply said, "That was so cool. But I don't have a testimony." You see, I had grown up hearing testimonies from a wide range of people: testimonies that turned into vocation stories, simple ways people have been radically changed, and the miracles written about in *By His Mercy*. I love hearing how God has worked in each person's life. I just don't have a radical story like that.

I grew up in a very Catholic family. Oh, I mean *very*. We went to Mass every weekend--I think I've missed Mass twice in my life; once we were snowed in (because, Minnesota) and the other time I was really sick. As kids, we were expected to go to confession once a month. We prayed family prayers together every night before bed. When I was 12, we moved into town to live a block away from our church. (I know, a young teenager's *perfect* dream.) At some point, we started praying the rosary on the mornings that we *didn't* go to daily Mass. Oh, and I was also homeschooled, which tends to be quite typical in a lot of Catholic families.

The Faith has always been a constant thing in my life. I couldn't tell you the first time I prayed the rosary, learned the Angelus, or read from my Bible. I could spout off facts about the Church like none other. I read stories about the saints... for fun. I knew my stuff, let me tell you that. But, if you had asked me why I did all the "faith stuff" that I did, I don't think I would have had an answer for you. It's just what I did. I loved my Faith, but I couldn't tell you why.

This involvement in my faith followed me all the way into high school (as did the homeschooling). I chose to attend monthly teen Lifeline Masses and weeklong Faith camps at the NET Center, Steubenville Conferences and Franciscan LEAD, and, after I got confirmed, helped as a small group moderator for Confirmation at my church. I went to all the Faith things and experienced the Lord each time. I would also get the "Jesus High" that came from those retreats.

I would go home and dive deeper, sometimes for two weeks and other times for six months. But, as I kept hearing other people's testimonies, I just felt stuck. I didn't have a cool story to share, so that must mean the Lord hadn't really worked in my life, right?

Along the way of attending all these things and, what seemed to be, diving into my Faith I actually realized that I didn't know why I was choosing all of it. Sure, my friends were all going to these retreats and conferences. I really did love praising Jesus and encountering Him through the events. I even liked sharing my Faith with others and trying to encourage them in their walk. But, why? Why did I love praising Jesus? Why did I want to encounter Him? Why did I want other people to love Him? Why did *I* want to love Him?

Over the course of a long time, (side note: Jesus does have a sense of humor when it comes to the impatient of heart) Jesus made me realize that all of it was done out of this overwhelming desire for something.

Sainthood.

Now, I'm not talking about the "recognized-by-the-Church-and-canonized" sainthood. I just want to get to Heaven and be with Jesus and the saints (hanging out with St. Papa JPII forever!).

The only problem is, I'm not really "saint material". I don't pray a ton. I'm not happy enough. I don't love enough and am pretty judgmental. I don't have enough patience. I make bad choices. I waste time on my phone. I fear dying and not getting to Heaven. I get super hyper and crazy sometimes. I tend to be very outgoing and loud in social settings. Basically, I am no Mother Teresa. I'm not even a young Karol Wojtyla (told you I know my saints). Oh, I also am not the most humble...whoops.

But, if I have only learned one thing from attending all those retreats, it is that there needs to be saints from this generation too. Saints that had cell phones, Instagram, and Snapchat. Saints that slept in too late on Saturdays and the extreme ones that traveled to Africa to show love. I am confident that this generation will have saints that accidentally pocket-dialed people or lived by the saying of, "Hot Spit." I believe this with all of my heart, because every single one of us has been called to this mission of sainthood. Just how we will be missionaries is different for each of us. I want to share the story of how Christ has called me to mission.

Let's rewind through a bit of my life story and go back to when I was about 14 or 15. I was a freshman or sophomore in high school and had been going to all the 'Faith things' for at least three years. I was invested and enjoyed going to everything, but I wanted a purpose for it all. Actually, I really wanted an overall purpose for my *faith*. I wanted an actual purpose because, at the time in my 14-year-old brain, sainthood wasn't a good enough purpose. So, I told Jesus that. Basically, I told Him, "Give me a tangible way to attain sainthood." Though I can assure you I did not use the word tangible. I don't think I even knew that word.

I can't distinctly tell you the moment when I finally became aware of the mission God was calling me to. It definitely wasn't one of those smack-you-upside-the-head-and-you-realize-what-God-wants-from-you moments. It was slowly and over a period of time. Again, Jesus wanted me to learn the virtue of patience. Again, I didn't (and still haven't!). Through what I was doing, be it participating in pro-life movements, helping friends through struggles they had, or watching medical drama TV shows, the Lord gave me my mission.

Save a life.

Okay, maybe that sounds cheesy to you. I mean, it still sounds cheesy to me too, sometimes. But, I want to explain, as best I can, why I believe God has given me this particular mission.

The first part is this: I do not know what kind of life the Lord wants to save through me. Maybe it is a physical life. I have felt a call toward entering the medical field and I could most definitely save a physical life through that. I have also been involved in the pro-life movement for as long as I can remember, and maybe a baby's life has been saved through that.

Maybe it is a mental life. I have always loved being the person that people come to when they are facing challenges and to help walk with them through it. I find beauty, and feel the love of God, in the fact that people choose me to be the one they come to when they need to talk. Sometimes the Lord gives me words to tell them, but, most of the time, I'm there to simply tell them, "Yeah, that really sucks. And I'm really sorry. But the Lord wants you to know that He loves you."

Maybe it is even a spiritual life I am meant to help save. I love sharing about my faith with others and encouraging them to let the Lord pursue them. The Lord has given me a fire to work in Youth Ministry and I may be able to be the person through whom teens encounter Jesus and ultimately save a spiritual life through that.

As I have gone through my high school years, I have had to decide what to do with my life and where I want to go. This mission to save a life has followed me through those decisions. Maybe it is even my own life the Lord has called me to save. I have had to dive deeper into my faith because of this call and have grown so much spiritually. I have been driven to learn how the human person works and how the brain functions, all because I want to be able to better respond to people. All the things the Lord has led me through to possibly help save another life has impacted my own life and possibly saved me from myself. I really do not know.

The second part of this mission is this: I will not know when, or if, I fulfill it. Until I get to the gates of Heaven, can look Jesus in the face, and ask, "Did I do it? Did I do the one thing you asked?", I will not know if I completed my work as a missionary for life. (He went at it again with the patience issue...). That means I can't stop trying. Wherever I am in life, whatever I am doing, and wherever I am going, I have to continue pursuing a saved life. All because Jesus has asked me to. This is the mission field He has placed me in.

Every single person that reads this book has also been given a mission. You and I truly are meant to be missionaries for the Lord. Whether you are a doctor, teacher, insurance agent, parent, sibling, anything, or anyone, the Lord calls you! He calls you to live life well and love Him. You don't have to have some crazy amazing encounter to have a testimony or even become a saint!

When Tricia first asked me to share my testimony for a second *By His Mercy* book, I was shocked. I honestly asked myself "What am I supposed to write about*?*" multiple times. I've heard about and seen miracle happens around me. I've witnessed people making complete 180° conversions. All my friends around me have amazing stories to share about how they have encountered God's mercy. Me? I've had a pretty average life, as you read above.

Now, I could have written about the few incredible experiences God has given me in Adoration. I could tell you of the countless mini-conversions the Lord has led me to over the course of my 18 years of life. I could even tell you about the multiple times He has radically used the Holy Spirit in and around me. But I really don't think that is why I was meant to share my story.

You see, the very same Jesus that may have given me an encounter with Him at a Steubenville Conference literally lives *within* you and me. The conversions I have been forced to have, because of my own turning away from Christ, is His way of saying "I love you", words that He tells you and me every single day. The Spirit that has radically changed my life and led me this far is just as present in your and my heart too, every day.

Sure, reading about miracles is incredible and can even increase our faith, if we let it. Reading about how God has worked is awesome and inspiring. But the stories, mission calls, and testimonies of love in this book mean nothing if we, both the writers and readers, do not answer the call of Love.

So yeah, my conversion story isn't the type of conversion story you would normally hear. Why? Because it is a story that has barely begun. As just a young, 18-year-old girl from Minnesota, each day that I wake up is both a continuation and a new beginning of my conversion. The Lord has been able to reveal to me that He works in smack-you-upside-the-head moments, but also in the quiet way of me choosing to get up and read my Bible, rather than roll over and go back to sleep in the morning. So, maybe you have one of those incredibly miraculous stories or maybe you have a story similar to mine. However, somehow, through the people God has placed in my life, I am realizing little by little that *each* of our stories is incredible, because they are Christ's.

So, I want to invite you to enter the battlefield of a life well lived with renewed courage, maybe even from reading this book. The Lord calls us each to sainthood through the everyday things we do; as I am just beginning to realize. I will save a life *through* living my life and you can love the Lord *through* letting Him love you. Wherever you are on your journey–nearing sainthood or having not even stepped on the path–He loves you. He sees you. He knows you. Will you let Him give you your mission?

Kate Shermach

"Pray without ceasing."

-1 Thessalonians 5:17

A time of sorrow began for my family in late 2014.

My husband, our two teenage daughters, and I had just taken a family vacation to the upper northwest to visit family. During the trip, we heard of the unrelated loss of two friends-one very young, and one of middle age. Although we enjoyed our vacation, we were all a bit out of sorts, and looking forward to getting home.

On our way home from Minneapolis/St. Paul airport, we received a call from my father-in-law in the Chicagoland area. One of the kindest, most gentle human beings I've ever known told us, on speakerphone, of the news that he was just diagnosed with lung cancer and was to be undergoing surgery within the next few weeks.

His surgery was a success, and the tumorous sections of his lungs had been removed. He had a tough recovery ahead, but we were all so relieved. A few weeks after his surgery, out of nowhere, his wife (my mother-in-law), suffered an intestinal blockage that required emergency surgery. Much of her large intestine was removed to save her life.

Sadly, she never came home. She suffered and passed away five weeks later in hospice. We were all numb. My husband took great effort in relocating his dad to the town where we live in western Wisconsin. We were all hopeful of the life we would share and how wonderful it would be to have dad living only five minutes away.

Our hopes were shattered within a few months. After given the "all clear" for his lung cancer, Dad's illness had spread to his brain. A stage- four, inoperable tumor took our hero from us almost a year to the day from losing my mother-in-law. My family was suffering so badly.

In a calendar year, we lost two parents, a sister-in-law, and yet another friend to long, agonizing, and ultimately futile battles. We were so weary of death, loss, hospitals, hospices, and were basically going through the motions in a state of hollow numbness to get through those first few days of 2016.

I remember my oldest daughter coming down with a cold the day after her grandpa died. She said it wasn't a big deal and didn't want to go to the doctor. We were all so sick of doctors. A freshman in college, she had a few weeks left of her Christmas vacation at home with us. Her 15-year old sister was already back at school. My husband was back to traveling for work again, and I was also back to work. We all had lots of healing to do. A new year was dawning.

Less than a week later, on January 13, 2016, I was getting ready for work. My husband was in Tennessee. Our oldest daughter was still fighting what seemed to be a bad cold, and so I had her sleep in my room with me in case she needed me in the middle of the night. We were all so tired of being in hospitals, and she was adamant about not going to the doctor. I told her to wake me up if she wanted to go in.

Instead, I couldn't wake her up.

It was surreal. I asked her if she wanted something to eat and if she was okay enough for me to go to work. She didn't respond. I sat by her on the bed and tried to wake her up. Nothing. I shouted out her name at her. Nothing. I shook her shoulders. Nothing. I fearfully peeled back her eyelid and what I saw was a vacant stare. Her forehead felt very hot, but thankfully I could feel her breathing. 911 kept me on the phone during the minutes it took for the ambulance to come.

Her fever was 106 degrees, and she was in a non-responsive state. After a spinal tap at our local hospital, it was determined that her condition was too severe for the scope of their care, and she was transferred to Regions Hospital in St. Paul, MN for specialized treatment.

I prayed and prayed like I had never prayed before. I was raised Catholic and have always been a believer in Christ. Although much of my adult life I had been distracted me from my Faith, the previous year had brought me closer to God. But no matter the depth of my belief, nothing could have prepared me for watching my daughter lying in a coma, under blankets of ice.

My husband was inconsolable. My youngest daughter was in shock. I started notifying my large extended family via phone calls and texts. Word spread quickly, but there was no encouraging news to share.

The doctors and nurses worked tirelessly. As one told me, "no one wants to see a teenager in the ICU". Countless tests were performed, and even the CDC tried to identify her condition. It was ultimately determined to be a rare strain of viral encephalitis. An untreatable diagnosis. Unknown was the strain of the illness, the cause, or the prognosis. I vowed to stay with my daughter in the hospital until the day she could come home. I didn't want her alone in case she awakened, and I wanted to be her voice and advocate to the medical professionals.

Many days passed. I prayed over her with the hospital. The hospital chaplain prayed with me. My sister, a hospice nurse and living angel, flew in to be with us at the hospital. She prayed with me. We set up a Caring Bridge page so more people could be kept up-to-date, and so they could pray for her. Silently she fought for her life, while we all prayed for her life.

My mom, a Third-Order Franciscan, started an international prayer chain. People all over the world were immediately praying for our girl as she lay there as still as death. Days dragged on and although nothing was changing, still we prayed. Through this poignant time of waiting helplessly, there was always prayer.

There were times while I was alone in her room, saying the Rosary at her bedside when I felt as though I was not alone. There was a divine presence there that gave me a sense of calm, a sense of peace, and most importantly, a sense of hope. It was a feeling I still can't describe other than that I knew we were not alone. It was as though I could feel the prayers of believers all over the world surrounding us and a silent voice telling me that it was going to be alright.

On day number eight, my husband and I were in her room, and being musical people, we played and sang familiar songs to her. A priest came and anointed her, and she had visitors. She lay there ever still, and we didn't know what was to come.

On the ninth day into her coma, our youngest daughter came running down the hallway on the ICU floor to find us. She was sure her big sister was fluttering her eyelids. We ran to her bedside and cried as this strong, beautiful, determined girl opened her eyes.

She was entirely unaware of what was happening, and hadn't come back into her mind yet. We continued our prayer with renewed hope and gratitude. Weeks passed, and she was still very much catatonic, and suffered physical atrophy, but was making improvement inches at a time. Her tracheostomy prevented her from any sort of speech, so we relied on other means of communication like using our eyes, or squeezing each other's hands. My husband and I were so grateful to have her alive that we were prepared for any version of our baby God would bless us with.

Did He bless us, indeed! Over the course of a few long months, she came back to us stronger than ever before. The sheer power of her spirit, strong will, and His grace lifted her up. Despite several weeks of total amnesia, she learned to walk and talk again. Her determination surprised the therapists and doctors.

The attitude she displayed still makes me cry to this day. Already a truly beautiful human being, she was so humbled by the odds she beat. She told me after she was home that she felt complete love during the times she remembered. Her gratitude in being given a second chance, and the determination to live out her dreams, has transformed this young woman. She has gained a perspective we could all learn from. Her spirit shines, and her smile is contagious.

Three years later, I still think about this experience every day. In my prayers, I always thank our Lord and Savior for bringing my girl back to us, and I am forever changed by this event. Little things that used to trouble me don't seem to matter anymore. Often, I still feel the presence of love I felt in that hospital room.

The prolific prayers of countless strangers are the greatest example of His love I have ever experienced. Life still has its challenges, but He taught me that even when life reveals its darkest times, I am not alone. None of us are.

Lucas Gerads

Just so, your light must before others, that they may see your good deeds and glorify your heavenly Father.

-Matthew 5:16

Growing up, I remember texting my mom once, " What religion am I?" It seems like such a weird question now because of how prominent it is in my life. I was raised Catholic but only in name really. I was baptized, went to religious ed, First Reconciliation and Communion, and Mass most Sundays. The faith was around me, just never the primary focus of life. Ya see, I was Sacramentalized and not Evangelized. So, my faith life was a rough total of two-ish hours a week on Wednesday night and Sunday mornings, assuming I went to both for a given week. The older I got, the stress on going to Mass lessened, and eventually we just stopped going except on Christmas Eve, Easter Sunday, and the occasional burst of energy to try and go more often. So for my childhood, I never really put my faith, belief, or trust in God.

So where does that leave me? When I entered seventh grade I was tired of being made fun of for my lack of athletic ability and weight, so I joined sports that I knew would be challenges for me and would prove my ability to others. Though challenging at first, cross country, swimming, and track and field did that for me. I gained a bunch of confidence and pride in my accomplishments and as a person in general. Out of the three sports, swimming was my main focus and the joy of my years. Having not been a swimmer before hand, I excelled at it, and in eighth grade, made the sections team. I was elected as the youngest Captain ever in my team's history at the end of my ninth grade year. Swimming had became the place that my identity rested in. When I did well, I was happy. When I had bad practices or meets, I was angry and upset. By the time sophomore year came around, the happiness, anger, excitement, and boredom of swimming had slowly started to leave me. I was left feeling empty and depressed. After that swim season, thoughts of suicide had already been entering into my head and a date was planned. Thank God that He had other plans.

Over the course of my sophomore year, I had been attending a non-denominational group called YoungLife. I went mostly to hangout with the friends I had from school, and during the talk about God, I zoned out. They eventually got me to sign up for a week long camping trip to Colorado in which I said would be my last moments before the aforementioned date. I left this thought at home though for hopes of finding a way out of my emptiness.

Amongst the Rocky Mountains of Colorado, we had an amazing trip filled with horseback riding, swimming, mountain biking, octaball, go-carts and good ol' hanging out. In between these activities we had little sessions and talks about Jesus, God, authentic love, mercy, and the works. I remember one moment vividly. The keynote was talking about the idea of God in Heaven with a tally board chalking up the good we do and the bad we do. Ultimately, I saw myself more on the bad side than the good. The lights went off and we watched the music video of Crowder's "Come As You Are." When it finished, a spot light came on the tally board and a hammer shattered it. We were told that we aren't a sum of our brokenness, or sin, but that we are beloved children of God. After this powerful message, we were invited to a time of silent prayer. In the darkness of the night sky in Colorado, I asked God to show me that He existed. At that moment, He called clouds to come over the surrounding mountains but leave the sky above us open. In the cloud, lightning started crackling all around. In the clear sky above me, shooting stars started to fly. I walked away in awe. I wish I could say that after that, I believed in God, but I wasn't convinced. So, the next night they invited us to a time of prayer again, and I asked the same thing. God once again showed me the power of His wonderful majesty over creation once again, and I remember saying, "Alright. I surrender."

On my way home, one of the leaders was asking about my experience and my life. He heard that I was Catholic and didn't know what to do with this new-found pursuit of God. This man led me straight to the Eucharist, where, for the first time, I felt the Divinity that was in the consecrated Host. He brought me to confession for the first time in 10 years, where I felt the pain and hurt caused by sin pool into my heart, and the hand of Christ reach into it and unravel it. This leader was a college student on a mission to lead others to Christ where he guided me to Him. Life hasn't been easy sailing since then, for being this conversion took place in 2013, and it's now 2019.

With every moment, I tried to keep Christ at the center of it all, and I did pretty well until college came. I attended St. Mary's

University of Minnesota in Winona, MN where I pursued a degree in Philosophy in the fall of 2015. Upon arriving, I found my community in Campus Ministry and the swim team. Even though I was quite active in Campus Ministry, I found myself being compelled in philosophy class and my thoughts starting to be changed by them. By the end of my freshmen year, I was starting to fall more frequently and not striving as much. I started to hangout with people who weren't supportive of the faith and led me away more. By the beginning of my sophomore year, I had little desire to practice my faith and fell into the party crowd, where I found myself in a life of sin. This life continued over the course of most of the year, and drained me of the joy I once felt in Christ. Being left once again empty, I found myself looking for help. Toward the end of April, I had a feeling to go and pray at the main chapel on campus, which was weird because I hadn't done that all year. But, having nothing else to distract me, I went. Entering, I had no clue what I was to pray about. So, I did something that I still could. I found a rosary and started praying. As I was praying, I felt a presence in the chapel, but didn't pay too much attention to it. By the second decade, this presence was behind me, with a hand on my shoulder. It's odd because nothing about this presence drew my attention, almost as if it didn't want it. By the third decade, the presence was directing its attention toward the Tabernacle and so then did I. I had looked at that Tabernacle many times and in that moment rays of light shone out of it like the sun. I believe that it was Mary there that night. Praying for me and with me. Guiding me toward her Son.

After that, I had made a promise to commit myself to Christ in all things and to follow Him even amongst the hardships of life. Shortly after my encounter on campus, the reality of not returning to Saint Mary's the next year set in. It broke my heart, but I just couldn't financially support my education at the place I had called home for two years. Upon returning to St. Cloud, I found myself lacking something that I took for granted while at Saint Mary's. Community. After having just recommitted myself to following Christ, I felt as if I was walking toward Him alone. In that struggle, I found myself invited to a Marmion house event. The Marmion house is a Catholic men's house for college students in St. Cloud that hosts events to build fraternal bonds in Christ. After just a few visits, Father Ben talked to me about moving in, and in January of that year, I did. We spent time playing pool, around bon fires, doing homework, and, most importantly, in prayer. As I longed for community, Christ led me to these men, and has blessed me abundantly through them. While in the house, I started to pray the Divine Mercy Novena leading up to Divine Mercy Sunday with the young lady who I was dating at the time. I had the intention of vocations through the nine days. Seeing a need for young men and women to courageously respond to the call of their vocations, I thought there would be no better way than through Divine Mercy. It was over these nine days that God had called back to my heart His request for me to enter Seminary. I was beyond confused. First off, I was dating an amazing women who led me toward Christ, and, secondly, I thought that I was for sure called to married life. But, through the course of the nine days, Christ continued to place the idea on my mind, while also breaking my heart. On Divine Mercy Sunday, I had finally surrendered to His will. In response to His call, though painful, I had to break up with the young lady I was dating, and started asking for the grace to follow Christ more relentlessly. I was asked to take a year for discernment purposes, and to go through the application process more fully. In this year the Lord has blessed me with many things. The opportunity to serve Him more at the altar, to minister to the youth, and homeless, and to deepen relationships. The most important growth though is in my relationship with God. He has revealed deep wounds and has been working in them. He has consoled me and left me in desolation. He has truly been the Good Shepherd to me through all that I have been involved in. This year is now entering into its final months, and while there is still much to do, I have started to ask for the grace needed to prepare my heart, mind, body and soul for Seminary. I'm beyond excited to see the growth in my relationship with Christ this coming fall (2019) as I will be entering the Immaculate Heart of Mary Seminary, but there is much to do and much growth to be had today and in the summer, so I continue to set my eyes on Him who leads me.

I find it fitting that this book is named *By His Mercy* for it has been only by His mercy that I'm here. He's led me the whole way though I tried to resist at times. He's always in pursuit of all of us, and wants nothing more than to shed His mercy upon us.

Theresa Lieser

"Fear not, I am with you; be not dismayed; I am your God. I will strengthen you, and help you, and uphold you with my right hand of justice."

-Isaiah 41:10

It was March of 2017. My husband, our three children, and I were excitedly embarking on a new adventure that God was leading us on. Knowing confidently that this was what He was asking us to do, we eagerly anticipated what was in store for us. All smiles, thumbs up, and ready to go in our vehicle, with two empty car seats waiting to be filled. Having only a few days of preparation, our family was about to grow from a family of five to a family of seven. For how long? Only God knew. We were ready to do this thing God was calling us to do. Trusting in His will.

Growing our family has never been easy. In fact, it has always been a challenge, testing our faith. It is a cross that we have learned to accept and carry. It is a cross that has deepened our own personal relationship with the Lord. It is a cross that has strengthened our love and marriage and has shown us that with God, anything is possible.

At the age of sixteen, after searching for an underlying cause to excruciating pain that I dealt with on a regular basis, it was discovered that I had a uterine abnormality that would someday make it difficult to carry a child in my womb. As devastating as it was to hear this news, I chose to move forward following my mother's advice to have hope, offer up my pain, and to trust God.

In the summer of 2005, I married my best friend at the age of twenty-one. As we discussed our future together, we chose to keep our Catholic faith and God at the center of our lives. We had witnessed in other marriages the beautiful fruits that bear as a result and wanted the same for ourselves. We chose to be open to life, but knew that if we were to have a family of our own someday, adoption may be the answer. God had other plans first.

Almost eleven months after we were married, we survived our first difficult pregnancy that had put our unborn baby's life in danger. Placing our child in God's hands, after fifteen weeks of strict bed rest, our daughter was miraculously born strong and healthy at thirty-five weeks. She had surpassed the twenty-eight week mark that doctors said we would likely not surpass! This new life, never needing any interventions whatsoever, showed us that incredible miracles can happen when you place your trust in Him. In a very scary, difficult time, we had found comfort together in our Lord while we lived the first major trial in our marriage. We had experienced for ourselves how fruitful it is when you place God and your faith in the midst of it all.

Sixteen months had passed when we surprisingly discovered that we were expecting our second little blessing. Though this pregnancy was not planned by us, it was planned by God and this child was most definitely loved and wanted. However, after carrying our baby within me for almost seven weeks, God took our little saint home to be with Him forever. This child will always hold a very special place in our family and forever will be imprinted on our hearts.

A few months later, we found ourselves expecting a third time. Again, placing our trust and our unborn child in God's hands, our son was born at thirty-seven weeks, strong and healthy! His life, too, was a testimony that faith can move mountains. In turning to God, He had given us all that we needed to survive another difficult, challenging pregnancy and time in our lives. He kept our son's life safe in His hands until he was in ours. Though our prayers were answered, we were about to face our biggest cross yet.

Praising God for this new life, with just minutes to meet and embrace our child that was just born, I was quickly rushed away. My own life was now in danger. My husband, holding our newborn son, was suddenly left alone standing in a pool of blood. As I was bleeding out, doctors unexpectedly had to perform an emergency partial hysterectomy to save my life. In an instant, I had almost lost my life, lost the ability to bear children, and had lost part of my womanhood. I was twenty-four years old. This was a sudden, tragic loss for us, and my faith was broken.

It was a very bittersweet time in our lives. As we rejoiced in this new life that we were blessed with, soaking in every single moment, we were also grieving the trauma and loss that we had just endured. Grateful that I was alive, and that we were blessed with two children on Earth, we knew our family was not complete, and the loss of part of my womanhood at such a young age was saddening for me. I had lost hope in the thought of any future children, and at times found myself angry at God, asking Him, "Why?". At other times, I sobbed uncontrollably at what had happened.

Weeks had gone by, when I found myself alone in my bedroom, tears streaming down my face. I didn't want to go through this loss. I didn't want to feel this anger, pain, and sadness anymore and wanted God to take it all from me. I turned to our Blessed Mother and asked her to please pray for me, begging her for these feelings to go away. Instantly, though no one else was around, I felt a long, warm, motherly embrace. My tears stopped flowing and it was as though they had been wiped away. I felt so much at peace and just knew that it was our Heavenly Mother comforting me.

I soon realized that the relationship that I had with the Lord was broken not because He left me, but because I had left Him. I realized that these feelings were not going to bring me closer to God, but would rather continue to separate me from Him. I knew that I needed to accept this cross, lay it at the feet of Jesus, and start mending what I had broken.

Taking the advice of a wise priest, I started asking our Lord daily to touch me with His healing hands and to help me carry this cross. I was tired and could not do it on my own. At times, when I fell into the sin of self-pity, I reminded myself that it wasn't about me, but about Him. We were enduring this cross for a reason and we needed to embrace it rather than turn away. If Jesus endured so much for us, couldn't I do this for Him?

Almost three years after our son's birth, with much healing and faith restored, we were just under a year into the infant adoption process when we were chosen by a birth mom. A month later, we welcomed our third child home! As God's plan for us was being revealed, we were overwhelmed by His abundant love and goodness.

I, a sinner, felt so undeserving of God's mercy, undeserving of our answered prayers. I felt wrong and ashamed for being so angry with Him. How could I have been so selfish? How could I have turned my back to our loving, Heavenly Father, Who only wants our love in return?

Another three years later, we felt God's call to adopt again. Two years into our adoption journey, nothing was ever working out. So many prospective adoptive situations came and went, and our faith was constantly being tested. Knowing in our hearts that our child or children were out there waiting for us, we knew that we were on the right path and couldn't give up. After being called by God to provide foster care as well, we finally responded and started the process.

With our adoption agency not having a foster care program, we turned to our county and received permission to be licensed with them while we worked with our agency. A few weeks before everything was final, we unexpectedly received a call for a foster placement. This was all quite unusual and very surprising as this call was not from our county, but rather our adoption agency.

A beautiful sibling pair of a six-month-old little boy and an almost three-year-old little girl was on their foster care journey and needed a new foster home. Their loving, biological grandparents were in search for a Catholic family able to care for them. After they were led to our agency, they found us. Our family instantly became fully on board and started preparing to welcome them into our home.

However, we learned quickly that God had other plans for us all instead. With distance and counties separating us all, they were not allowed to move to our county. With that, as they moved on to another foster home, we had to move on as well.

Four months later, having had the privilege of loving two other foster babies, we sadly said our goodbyes and watched them move on. Around the same time, God again placed several prospective adoptive situations in and out of our lives. With broken hearts, we were tired and needed rest from the roller coaster of emotions. We just didn't know how much more we could handle and wanted to know why God was leading us down this path.

After taking a little break from it all, together as a family, we were ready to step back in and give it one more chance. The day before we made the call to our county to let them know, we once again were contacted by our adoption agency regarding the same little boy and girl we were asked to care for five months prior. God had placed them back into our lives! Their loving biological grandparents had not given up. They had persevered in prayer and encouragement to move the children to us, and as a result, their county had finally agreed.

Ourselves having lost some faith along the way, fear of the unknown settled in our minds. "What if they don't attach? What if they do attach and they have to leave? What if they are too difficult and have behaviors we just cannot handle?" We quickly were fully confident that it was not God's will for us to care for them and said "no" to caring for them. We turned them away.

The following day, things did not feel right. I didn't feel as confident as I had felt the day before about refusing to take these two children in. Different questions started racing through my mind. "What if they need us? What if it is God's will for us to love and care for these two little ones? What if they are our children that we have been waiting and searching for? What if they are the answer to our prayers?" My mind became restless, so I decided to turn to our Lord in the Blessed Sacrament in Adoration, hoping to find an answer.

Sitting there with God in Church, I asked Him to show us what He wanted us to do. It suddenly occurred to me that we only knew these two children's first names. Instantly feeling a strong urgency to know their middle names, I quickly sent a message to find out.

Waiting for a response, I felt in my heart that if one of them had a middle name that we had planned for any future children of ours, then it was God's will for us to care for them. I thought to myself how silly this was and that there was no way they had a name we had picked out. Not expecting a quick reply, I opened up the message while sitting in the presence of Jesus.

Upon reading the answer, my jaw dropped instantly in disbelief. The little girl had the same middle name as mine and it was the one we had chosen as a middle name for a future daughter. It was in that moment that I knew what we had to do. After telling my husband, we realized that we had to say yes as this was God's will for us all.

A few days later, in March of 2017, our hearts were ready to bring them home and we were on our way. When we did, it was as if they had been with us all along. They were the missing pieces to our family that we had been searching for and they were finally here with us. God had brought seven people together in a unique and miraculous way. Though we all had our issues and were broken in different ways, each of us were healing towards one another.

In November of 2018, after nineteen months of sharing our love and home with them, not knowing what the future held, we finally were able to officially welcome them into our family as we finalized their adoption. Our hearts joyfully overflowed with God's abundant love!

Looking back, I'm overwhelmed by the Lord's strong presence through it all. He was there every step of the way, never leaving us. In times when we felt alone, it was not because He wasn't present; it was because we had turned away. He allows crosses in our lives so that we can grow closer to Him. He waits for us to bring Him our struggles because we cannot do it on our own. He pours love on us daily, wanting nothing but our love and friendship in return. No matter what life brings us, He will always give us what we need to get through it all. Just imagine the amazing fruits He has waiting for you if you just invite Him in more!

James Uthmeier

*All God asks of you is this: to act justly, love tenderly,
and walk humbly with Him.*

- Micah 6:8

Want to live all in? Make life a pilgrimage.

It was about midnight, I had not slept in over thirty-six hours, and I was starving... in both a physical *and spiritual sense*, though perhaps I did not yet know it. I had spent all day traveling from the United States to Rome to begin a summer work assignment, and the hours of travel delays, customs issues, and wrong-turns had taken their toll. I arrived long after midnight at my summer accommodations, a generous Catholic seminary located just outside of the heart of Rome. It would not be until the next day that I would learn that the seminarians had waited up many hours in an attempt to give me a warm welcome and home-cooked Italian dinner. They don't get too many foreign visitors who are not wearing a collar. But now they were all asleep—the campus was dark, silent, and sealed by what appeared to be a ten-foot wall. The front gate, made of thick iron, was securely locked.

As I gazed up at the concrete barrier, which looked twice as ominous under the glow of the moonlight, my stomach sank. It was but another huge obstacle in what felt like a never-ending day of travel. As I checked the address for the third time, to make sure I was at the right place, a sarcastic but optimistic voice cracked up behind me, "looks like you are going to have to climb hermano!" My travel colleague, one of Guatemala's brightest law students, seemed to take pleasure in our predicament. "Oh yeah, that's the right address," he chided, "looks like you're going to see what it's like for my people south of your border who try to climb over in peril." Yes, that is close to a direct quote. I gave him a shove, but I could not help but grin. This would be the first of many days that I would experience Javier's politically incorrect humor, but his always-optimistic spirit gave me the encouragement I needed to keep going.

It was June 2012. Javier and I were traveling to Rome as part of a legal internship program that connects Christian law students from around the world with faith-focused summer jobs. The program presents a terrific opportunity for law students to unite with hundreds of other bright, like-minded students and dedicate a summer to service before beginning professional careers. Perhaps most importantly, it also provides meaningful time to discern vocation and assess how we could use our God-given talents to change the world. The fact that a beach boy from Florida and big-city Guatemalan would develop a lifelong friendship exemplifies the reach and beauty of the program. Neither of us knew that we would be assigned to work in Rome prior to committing our summer. It was simply the Holy Spirit, and it would change both of our lives forever.

Okay, back to the story. Javi and I took a deep breath, tossed our bags over the wall, and prepared to climb. But just as he planted a foot into my clasped palms and I began to hoist upward, a light illuminated on the other side of the wall and a voice from afar reassured us that help was on the way. I don't remember which seminarian drew the short straw to wait up for us, but we were certainly grateful.

After a long escort through the maze of dark pathways on the seminary grounds, we finally made it to our humble accommodations—air-condition-less dorms, firm beds, and small confines equipped with nothing more than a prayer kneeler and bible. Despite the balmy Roman summer weather, sleep may have overcome me that night before my head hit the pillow.

The next morning Javi and I stumbled out bleary-eyed and consumed by jet lag and trudged towards the seminary's dining quarters. A distant gong! had awoken us to the call for breakfast. He greeted me with a friendly handshake and jolly laugh as we linked up in the dorm hallway.

We were eager to meet the seminarian "brothers" with whom we would live during our time in Rome. As we entered the dining hall, hundreds of men, all clothed in the same short-sleeve white button-up shirts, black slacks, and tightly groomed haircuts sat eating their food in silence. We sat down behind two unclaimed plates, made the sign of the cross, and began eating. Oddly, the room remained silent. Javi, being a friendly Latino, attempted to introduce himself to a few of the Hispanic brothers sitting at our table. They shot a few polite nods but did not say a word. We glanced at one another, shrugged, and succumbed to the silence. Such a strange welcome!

A short time later, after a cue that I clearly missed, the men stood simultaneously, in regiment, said a quick prayer in Spanish, and abruptly left the room. Perplexed, Javi and I quickly finished our coffee—which, I must mention, was an absolutely breathtaking Italian roast that I will never forget. As we departed the dining hall in search of someone in charge, a tall seminarian came jogging up to us. He was clearly one of the few Americans on campus, and we could tell by his warm grin and eager jaunt that he was expecting us. That would be our first interaction with the future Father Mark.

Brother Mark apologized for the confusing welcome and explained one of the many rules of seminary life—breakfast in silence—which we would grow to enjoy. The time is designated for prayer, reflection, and peaceful preparation for the day. There is a power in silence, especially amidst the busy noise and commotion of every-day life, that is key to maintaining a well-nurtured and faith-filled spiritual life.

Mark gave us a quick tour of the grounds, overview of seminary rules, and a promise that we would have an epic summer. He assured us that the transformative beauty of Rome would captivate our hearts. After giving us a few other tips, he then pointed us in the direction of the legal office where we would meet our boss and get to work. Our summer jobs would prove to be fun and rewarding, but that is not what made the summer so special, or the focus of the chapter.

The next night I was awakened from a deep sleep by an unexpected 5:30 am knock on the door. I stumbled from the bed to the familiar voice of Br. Mark. "James, get dressed quickly, we are going to see Saint Peter." Still assessing whether I was dreaming, I wondered if this activity was optional. I had not signed up for this. What did he mean, *see* Saint Peter? Surely none of the churches in Rome were even open this early. But my curiosity was piqued and I decided to check it out. Little did I know that my decision to say "yes" that morning, and shake my slumber, was a new beginning—

the spark of a desire to live all in. I threw on a clean polo, splashed some water on my face, and darted out the door.

Like clockwork, Javi was rushing out of his dorm room at the same time. I was glad that he had also responded affirmatively to the invitation. "What time is it, Gringo?" he remarked. I didn't have time to respond before Br. Mark ushered us into a small European car and away we zipped towards the heart of Rome, Vatican City.

As we tucked into a tight parking spot on a narrow, cobblestone road, the sun began to peak over the horizon. We had only walked a few short blocks before I recognized our destination. I had never before seen her in person – before me stood the most magnificent church. Softly glowing under the rising sun, as she does so brilliantly in the early morning, the façade of St. Peter's Basilica commanded the sky.

A combination of soaring pillars, strong symmetrical lines, semicircular arches, and a breathtaking hemispherical dome made evident that this was the largest church in the world—fitting for the chair of Saint Peter. Words cannot do it justice. The basilica appeared even larger resting behind an empty St. Peter's square—one of Bernini's famed architectural designs—centered by an ancient Egyptian obelisk. Tall colonnades surrounded the circular plaza like outstretched arms beckoning pilgrims from all directions toward the church's entrance.

Arriving at the obelisk, still unable to take my gaze from the Basilica, I thanked Mark for bringing us here. "What an incredible way to see her for the first time," I told him. He responded, "You have not seen anything yet!" still taking delight in the secrecy of what was in store for us. I glanced at my watch to see that it was not quite 6:00 am. Knowing that the church did not open for visitors for another three hours added to the shroud of mystery.

Three people approached us in the square, evidently planning to meet us. The first was a priest who seemed to know Br. Mark. But he looked just as tired as Javier and I and equally as confused about the purpose of our visit. Little did he know that he would have the greatest treat of the morning! The other two individuals were a young adult couple. Their English made clear they were from the United States. They did not need to tell us they were on their honeymoon—constant smiles and a warm glow surrounded them as they too gawked at the surreal landscape around us.

We did not have long for a greeting. Mark told us we had to hurry, and we all raced quickly to the Basilica. I would later learn that a morning like this was not uncommon for Fr. Mark. Hundreds of people from across the U.S. are connected to him when they visit Rome, and he shares with them perhaps his greatest gift—we'll get to that. Nearing the Basilica we were stopped by a security checkpoint and secured gate. *I knew the church was closed*, I thought to myself, *why are we here?* But in surprising fashion Mark muttered some Italian to the guards, they nodded, and we were ushered past the gate. We climbed the imposing steps and entered the empty sanctuary.

An empty Saint Peter's is a sight like no other. Cruciform in shape, the elongated sanctuary seems to stretch for miles (running the length of two American football fields!). The greatest of all churches in Christendom, she is adorned in marble, embellished with copious renaissance decorations, and majestic statues of angels and saints line the walls and ceiling above. As much as I wanted to stop to admire Michelangelo's famous *Pieta* statue of Mary holding Jesus, Br. Mark dragged us deeper into the church. We ran past the tombs of popes and under the shadow of the famous Bernini baldacchino sculpture, a 9-story bronze structure that tents the center altar. Its four spiraling columns, garnished with gold decorations, rose to a sculpted bronze canopy—a floating appearance that draws all eyes up to Michelangelo's dome and heaven above.

Supporting the central edifice of the sanctuary are four heavy marble buttresses that serve as primary bases for the sweeping arches that support the dome and ceiling of St. Peter's. To call them mere columns would do an injustice to their size. Each houses a large statue depicting one of the four evangelists and tradition holds that preserved deep within are the spear that pierced Jesus, cloth that wiped His face, wood from the true cross, and relics of St. Peter. Br. Mark headed straight for one of these structures and motioned for us to follow. Sure enough, dwarfed at the base of the column was a small door guarded by a lone Vatican security guard. As we approached, he recognized Br. Mark and stepped aside to let us pass.

Through the door we scurried down a narrow spiraling staircase into the depths below. I felt the temperature drop as we descended into a crypt of sorts. Several stories lower we reached the bottom. A dimly lit stone paved path awaited us. We walked down the corridor, passing small grottos and chapels on our right and left. I could tell we had reached our destination when Br. Mark stopped and his knees hit the ground. The five of us fell to the floor behind him as we entered the Clementine Chapel. "Behind that altar rests St. Peter," Mark whispered.

While we celebrated Mass in the chapel barely large enough to fit our small contingent, I felt my Catholic faith reinvigorated. The teaching was no longer mere text on paper. It no longer felt like only lofty sentiments and noble doctrine. In that moment the faith was real to me. I could see it, I could touch it. My senses were consumed and my full attention captured. As our small congregation recited the Creed, the prayer struck me like never before—*We believe in one, holy, catholic, and apostolic Church.* Praying with the remains of Peter just feet in front of us, my eyes turned upwards. Br. Mark saw my gaze. "Yes James, we are directly beneath the main altar above ... the center of the Church." The words of Matthew rang through my head. "And I say to you that you are Peter, and upon this rock I will build My church."

As Father raised the host for consecration, I felt such an appreciation for the universality of the Church and communion of saints. The Eucharist was not and is not just some made up fiction. It was not an invented ritual. Rather, this is what Jesus taught us—what he gave us and continuously gives to us at the altar. That morning I not only received the Eucharist along with Father, Br. Mark, Javi, and the newlyweds. I received in communion with St. Peter; St. John Paul II, lying nearby in St. Peter's main sanctuary; countless Popes buried around us; and all of the apostles and saints who dedicated their lives to building the universal Church.

I spent hours upon hours in St. Peter's Basilica that summer exploring the art, praying in silence, and learning about her history. The hard-to-get Vatican "Scavi Tours" take pilgrims deep beneath St. Peter's, where an underground necropolis (*i.e.* ancient cemetery) tells the story of Peter's martyrdom. As most know, Peter was crucified upside down inside the Emperor Nero's Circus, a stadium that neighbored a hill known as *Vaticano.* The stadium served as entertainment to the Romans. Sadly, an element of that entertainment was often the brutal killing of Christians by fire, combat, and crucifixion. Peter's crucifixion took place near an ancient Egyptian obelisk. Today that obelisk stands in the center of the square.

What many do not know is that Peter's remains, like many of the early Christian martyrs, were taken just outside the stadium and buried at a site near the edge of Vatican Hill. The location had been a place of burial for hundreds of years. Here, other Christians would come to pay homage and visit their predecessors, often risking their own lives to do so. People would travel from far away to bury loved ones near Peter, knowing that when Jesus would come again, he would surely come for Peter.

About 300 years later, after the Emperor Constantine's conversion, he built an Old St. Peter's basilica over the burial ground. Constantine leveled Vatican Hill to create a flat foundation for his Basilica. In doing so, he covered *and thus preserved* the remains of St. Peter and the early Christians. Another 1200 years later, a new St. Peter's Basilica was constructed on top of the old one, further burying the necropolis and its story. The notion that the Basilica was built on top of Saint Peter would become a tradition, and many would forget what actually lies below. It would take another 750 years for excavations to reveal the well-preserved remains. Hundreds of gravesites, carvings, and meaningful clues pointing to something special—the bones of St. Peter secured deep and directly below the center alter. He was right there the entire time.

Exiting St. Peter's Basilica that first morning I gazed out at the gargantuan 300-ton obelisk in the middle of the square. It dawned on me that this sight—the obelisk—was likely the last thing Peter saw before he died. It serves as a perfect symbol of his witness, and a nice reminder to all those leaving the church as they go back into the world.

The summer pilgrimage in Rome changed my life. It took me outside of myself and outside of my normal patterns of everyday living. Even Catholics who attend weekly Mass and practice the sacraments can fall into complacency and just "go through the motions." The Rome pilgrimage shook me up and energized me to inward reflection and reexamination of life priorities. I felt God calling me to continue pilgrimaging.

Br. Mark, Javi, and I had quite a summer. We were part of a living history. We walked the streets of saints and martyrs. We learned the stories of the artists that dedicated their lives to works of art—they believed it was their ticket to heaven. We trudged through the Vatican, Coliseum, and Roman Forum. Renowned art historian and guide Elizabeth Lev led us through the renaissance plazas and churches hidden in the backstreets of Rome. Countless churches serve as the living witness to the faith of saints and artists—San Ignazio, Il Gesu, San Luigi dei Francesi, Santa Maria Sopra Minerva, San Andrea in Quirinale, and so many others. We visited old friends buried in the catacombs and celebrated Mass with the man that succeeded Peter in leading almost a billion believers. We couldn't get enough. Travels to nearby Sienna, Florence, Venice, Assisi, and other Italian towns reaffirmed that holy places of witness are not solely within Rome—they are scattered around the entire world!

As much as we did not want the summer to end, it did. But the pilgrimage did not. We could not wait to share our experiences with others, and the Holy Spirit had a plan.

* * *

Fast forward two years later and I found myself again hearing the call to pilgrimage. This time it was a bit more direct. Father Mark, who was now a newly ordained priest, had recently led several wealthy adults on pilgrimage. He called to tell me about it. Recognizing that nine out of ten pilgrims were seniors finally making the most of well-earned savings and free time, Father expressed frustration. Why did these people have to wait for retirement to discover the beauty of their faith on pilgrimage? Why couldn't choosing a career, a job, a spouse, discerning a vocation become part of a journey, a pilgrimage? Father exclaimed that young people too must discover the beauty and depth of life, faith, and tradition. And it would be great if they could experience these gifts earlier rather than later.

Initial fundraising was easy. Parents that learned life's lessons the hard way were eager to create opportunities for young people, like their children, to pilgrimage through Christianity's history alongside other young adults and professionals. As Fr. Mark and I began fundraising, early benefactors compared our idea to the Jewish Birthright program, a widespread philanthropic effort to fund Israel trips for young people of Jewish decent. *Why are there no birthright programs for Christian young people?* We had to do something.

As Fr. Mark and I began thinking about young adult pilgrimages, one thing became clear. There were virtually no opportunities, especially in the U.S., for young people to go on pilgrimage. While many church parishes organized them, they were expensively overpriced and focused on a more "comfortable" experience for seniors and retirees. Moreover, young people have a different, more engaging experience when they are encountering sacred places together with other young people. We wanted to create a network of young people, across the world, through pilgrimage. Father hit the ground running with the recruitment and organization of some quick trips. He needed my help *fast!* He charged me to build a nonprofit organization that could make everything happen. Legal documents, financing, and developing relationships with travel suppliers and young adult ministries, those were some of my assignments.

Today I do not quite remember why there was a need for urgency (other than saving souls, of course). Perhaps it was simply Father's priestly desire to move forward with the same energetic passion that fueled the Apostles—a feeling that time cannot be wasted. There was just one problem, I had to take the legal bar exam the very next month, and my time was already spread thin. It was the last hurdle standing between me and a license to practice law.

Unlike most of my colleagues who had been buried in the books for months, I was not able to begin studying until just weeks before the exam. Limited funds and a summer job delayed and distracted my preparations. I even moved back in with my parents in order to focus the final few weeks of July on the bar. However, Father Mark made clear that we could not wait another month—the time was now! I too felt called to begin building the nonprofit organization immediately. And thus the Pilgrim Project was born, a nonprofit corporation dedicated to transforming young adults through pilgrimage. Despite my lack of bar prep, and the fact that I was already risking a failing score, I worked tirelessly to get the Pilgrim Project officially off the ground. "Don't worry about the bar exam," Father would remind, "it's going to be just fine." If only he were the one taking it, I would often think to myself. He was right.

The bar exam is a two day exam. It is riddled with confusing hypotheticals, tests of arcane rules, and complex scenarios that quiz analytical reasoning and logic. Many view it as one of the most difficult tests of knowledge and critical-thinking. I was unprepared, and I knew it immediately after turning the first page. There were subjects I had never studied, concepts I had long forgotten. I read through the multiple essay questions that make up half the exam. I felt like my multiple choice performance—the other half of the exam—was probably good enough to hit the 70% passage mark... thus it would all come down to the essays. Some questions prompted me to remember partial answers, but surely not enough to secure a passing score.

Question after question, I began to panic. *Would my law firm job offer still stand? How would I tell my parents? Would I really have to take this dang test again?* My mind started to wander, and I turned to prayer. Then, I flipped to the last essay question on the bar exam, a hypothetical: A wealthy individual passed away leaving a large amount of money to a religious organization with the direction to establish a nonprofit and foundation for charitable efforts. What was the legal analysis? Jackpot. I knew the topic back and forth thanks to the Pilgrim Project. I still remember when I saw my passing score. God had been on my side, and I passed by the skin of my teeth. I promised Him in that moment that I would not take my gift for granted and would use it to give back.

A year later, I was back in Rome. But this time I was with 25 young adults from 7 different countries. Latinos, Europeans, and Americans, we were all there together. We celebrated Mass at St. Peter's, walked single file through the winding passageways of the underground catacombs, and enjoyed the wine, pasta, history, and everything else that Rome has to offer. Late night discussions and the power of joint experiences—*living the faith together*—bridged continents and built bonds of friendship greater than I could have imagined.

I saw numerous young men and women from different backgrounds and upbringings experience the same converting beauty that captured my heart three years prior. Many of these individuals may never have had such opportunities but for the financial assistance and work of the Pilgrim Project. Witnessing these gifts has served as a meaningful reward for the Project's growing team of volunteers who continuously make pilgrimage possible for young adults.

The Pilgrim Project has led many unsuspecting young adults to Rome who are unaware of the miracles they may experience through pilgrimage. Year after year, a young person enters RCIA and joins the Catholic Church after completing a pilgrimage. Some have discerned vocations. Others have rededicated themselves to the faith and have even begun new ministries of their own. All have had a lot of fun—*yes*, pilgrimages are fun!

Our dream of a network of young pilgrims spread across the world was becoming a reality. But Rome was just the beginning. Other holy places were beckoning us to lead young people on pilgrimage: Lourdes, Fatima, Guadalupe and the Marian shrines; Jerusalem and the Holy Land, where pilgrims see Sacred Scripture come to life as they, *quite literally*, walk in the footsteps of Jesus; the Catholic monasteries of France, major influences on Western Culture;

and St. Thomas More and the English martyrs' witness to the importance of the sacraments—namely, marriage.

Just when I thought that I had experienced all of the gifts of pilgrimage, God surprised me yet again. A year after Fr. Mark and I set out on our journey, the challenges of planning international travel for dozens of young people proved to be too much. We needed the assistance of an expert. A small travel company in Detroit offered to lend us a hand. Jean, a tenured travel agent who focused on pilgrimage tours, was assigned to be our account manager. She shared our passion for pilgrimage like no other, and embodied our burning desire to create engaging, transformational experiences for young people.

Jean would play hard to get for a couple years, but on a Pilgrim Project New Years pilgrimage to Rome she would realize that I was her person. We were engaged a year later and visited Rome as newlyweds the following, again on a pilgrimage. Thanks to the help of an old friend, we were able to meet Pope Francis and receive a Papal marriage blessing in our wedding attire. After years of carrying pilgrims' backpacks and souvenirs through St. Peter's Square, carrying my bride through the plaza was a nice change.

Want to live all in? Make life a pilgrimage. Twelve poor fishermen set off on foot and changed the world. They built the Church we have today. And to think, they did it without the backdrop of the pilgrimage sites and history that we have at our disposal.

Glorious examples of Christ's love for the Church surround us—holy places where the apostles, disciples, and saints heroically responded to God's calling. I assure you, pilgrimage is the new evangelization. Get away from the noise and many daily distractions, and you might just find what God has in store for you.

For the Church, pilgrimages, in all their multiple aspects, have always been a gift of grace.

-St. John Paul II

Mary Solarz

*"He will swallow up death forever. The Sovereign LORD will
wipe away the tears from all faces; he will remove his people's
disgrace from all the earth. The LORD has spoken. In that day they
will say, "Surely this is our God; we trusted in him, and he saved us.
This is the LORD, we trusted in him; let us rejoice and be glad
in his salvation."*

-Isaiah 25:8-9

Everybody dies and is born to eternal life. Ever since I was a little kid, I have known this. But it never really clicked in my head or really sunk in. When I was young, I remember going to wakes and funerals of people whom my family knew from the neighborhood or were family friends, but I was fortunate that at that point in my life I had never lost someone who was close to me. Some of you today are in the same shoes I was before the sixth grade; you have never lost someone close and dear to you. But, on the other hand, most of you have lost a grandparent, an aunt, an uncle, a sibling, and maybe even a parent. I know what you are going through. But then, March 18, 2006 my grandma was born to eternal life.

It was just a normal day in February; I was doing my homework after school and my mom was helping me as usual. All of a sudden the phone rang. It was the hospital calling for my mom. The secretary told my mom that my grandparents were in the ER due to a car accident. My grandpa was doing well; he just had a couple of scrapes and bruises. But as for my grandma that was another story. She was injured much more severely than my grandpa. My mom hung up the phone and the look on her face told me that something was very wrong, even though she would tell me at the time was that we just have to go and visit grandpa and grandma, not wanting me to worry.

When we got to the hospital, I remember seeing a bag at the side of the gurney that was full of clothes that were my grandparents' and they were all full of blood and cut up. A million questions bombarded my mind. Later that day we finally saw grandma and I sobbed, just the sight of her in pain was very hard. My grandpa got to go home that day, but grandma had to stay because how serious her condition was.

My grandma stayed in the hospital until the day she died. My mom and her siblings called Fr. Mark, our local priest, a few days before she died to give her Last Rights. The night before my grandma died, she started getting better and was transferred out of the ICU. We were amazed and thought that she would get through this. But the next morning, Grandma coded-a code blue. Code blue means that the heart stops due to a blood clot going to the heart. Grandma was unresponsive. My family was standing outside the door, and we were crying and praying. Our hopes soared again when the doctors, with the help of the nurses, revived my grandma.

Later that night, Grandma coded again. My mom and her siblings needed to decide whether to have the doctors try to revive her again or let her be with God. My mom and her siblings decided to try to revive her one last time. This was a hard decision to make due to how much pain she was in. Later that night, her vitals started to drop to a dangerous level. The doctor said my grandma had a low chance of survival. Eventually my mom and her siblings said their goodbyes and set my grandma free. My cousin, Michelle, and I were the only grandkids who saw my grandma before she was set free. By this time I was crying. I didn't want to say good bye to grandma, and desperately wanted her to be here in the morning when I woke up. The next morning I was told the news: Grandma was gone. I was so angry at God.

I kept asking myself why God would do this to me, and I kept thinking that He was punishing me for some reason. I started to shun God from my life. As the days went on, I was losing my faith. I still attended Mass because my parents wanted me to, but I really wasn't paying attention because and my heart was closed off from God. If God took someone that I loved so dearly, why should I pay attention to His messages? After a while, though, I started to pray more, I became involved with the church more, and it made me feel that I was getting a little closer to God again.

About two years after my grandma died, I attended my first Steubenville Youth Conference. During Adoration on the second night of the conference, I started to pray and was thinking about my grandma. I blocked out all distractions all around me, and then all of a sudden everything went white. Then I saw an image of my grandma and God walking together in heaven. That image he gave me let me know that my grandma was happy, and he also let me know that I could talk to her any time I wanted. Then it hit me: I knew why God called my grandma home. It was just simply her time to go home; God had better plans for her in Heaven. Here God and I strengthened our relationship together. My faith was strengthened tremendously through this experience.

I became very active in youth group, going on numerous retreats. I started a prayer group for priests and seminarians that continued until I was a senior in high school. I became a Mass server until my senior year of high school, and I helped train in the new servers. I became a member of the choir, and a cantor. After confirmation I became a Eucharistic minister, lector, and a religious education teacher.

I didn't realize how much the death of my grandma would impact how I dealt with the passing of my dad in 2017. I always knew that I would lose my dad at a young age, due to him being very sick with congestive heart failure, kidney failure, and Chronic Obstructive Pulmonary Disease. But there was always hope that he would be able to watch me succeed in my career as a social worker, or if God was calling me to married life to walk me down the aisle and give me away, or if I was called to religious life to see me take my final vows.

When I was a sophomore in college, my dad had frequent hospital stays. As a family we needed to make the hard decision if dad should start dialysis. Dad agreed to try it for a couple of years. I could see how much toll the dialysis took on him, and towards the end, after receiving dialysis three times a week for about four years, my dad was ready to pass away from this life and go on to the next. I remember the last week of my dad's life well, and I was happy that I was able to spend the time with him that I did. . The night before my dad's death, after dialysis, my dad was very lethargic, leaning to one side, and not really responding. The workers at the dialysis unit thought he suffered a small stroke, so he was sent to the ER. That night, dad was admitted because he had an infection in his blood, and was not getting enough oxygen into his blood stream. Both my mom and I we went home just thinking that this would be another hospitalization and dad could be here for a while. The next morning, we received a call from the hospital saying that his oxygen saturations were low. We rushed to the hospital. When we got there, my dad was given Last Rites and my mom and I were able to be with him when he took his last breath.

November 11th will always be a hard day for me. I can still remember sitting with my dad, holding his hand, and giving him permission to be with God. At first, I was jealous of my half siblings. They had known dad longer and were able to spend more time with him. But I soon realized that I had spent quality time with him too. He was a stay- at- home parent and was always there when I needed him. I will always hold on to the lessons that he taught me. It has been over a year now, and I can tell that my dad is watching over me. I can still hear his advice in my head, and when I come across his favorite TV shows it brings back fond memories of me watching them with him. It always makes me smile!

Dad's funeral will always hold a special place in my heart. I was able to serve at the funeral Mass even though it had been years since I served at Mass. He was always proud to see me serving, so it meant a lot to me to be able to do that for him. . Something that I will never forget was that the funeral director let me drive the hearse to his final resting spot, and my mom accompanied me as well. It was a blessing to have a final moment together as a family before we laid him to rest. We even got to drive past the house, the place where my dad had built a family home so full of love for my mom and I.

A couple of months after my dad's death, I was struggling with depression and grief. I was very mad at God for taking him. But I was also at peace because my dad was ready to go home, and he no longer had to suffer and be weak after dialysis. One day, I decided to visit his grave. While I was there I was praying for the repose of his soul, and I asked God to give me the opportunity to hear his voice again. About five minutes later my phone dinged, and I had a missed voicemail. To my amazement, it was a voicemail from my dad a couple months earlier. Instantaneously I began to cry. Just hearing his voice, I knew everything would be okay and that the depression and grief would get easier.

December 2018 into January 2019, I had the opportunity to go to Rome with the Pilgrim Project, and the hope of this retreat was so I could actually give myself time to grieve the loss of my dad. I hadn't really processed his death; the whole week of the wake and funeral had been a blur, and since then I had just focused on going about my day and always stayed busy. While in Rome, I made the consecration to Jesus through Mary, and since then I have had a deeper connection with our Blessed Mother. She has helped me through my depression and grief, as she went through the same thing when her only Son was crucified. I also felt called to light a candle in memory of my dad at St. Paul's Outside the Walls, in Rome, and I again asked God to give me a sign just to let me know everything was okay and that my dad was in heaven. God once again fulfilled my request, also in the form of a voicemail. . But in this particular voicemail, my dad told me to be safe and he told me that he loved me. To this day, God surprises me with little things to help me remember that my dad is always around, and that he is in heaven watching over and praying for me.

Life hits us with many obstacles that may seem impossible to overcome. But God knows that He will help us through them, only by His grace. All he asks is that we love and trust in Him so that He can set us free from all the pain and burden in our lives. The death of my grandpa was a blessing in disguise that God gave me. It made me a stronger as a person, it made me understand why God calls people home, and it prepared me for the death of my father in 2017. I got involved in the church, and more importantly it gave me a better, stronger, relationship with God. When we allow God to take control of our lives He sets us free to live a truly blessed and happy life.

Sarah Dvoracek

"Be still and know that I am God."

-Psalm 46:10

This is a story of childish faith, overcome by God's great love. My entire life, God has continued to show His great love for me by working in radical ways. I would like to start by sharing some of the countless examples.

When I was just a few months old I had congenital glaucoma. This is a rare condition in which fluid did not drain from my eyes. If untreated, I would lose my eyesight. An expert in congenital glaucoma happened to be in my hometown at the time it was discovered and after two emergency surgeries I have almost no damage to my eyesight.

I grew up in a loving Catholic family, who always took me to church and invested time in my Catholic education. When I was ten, I was at a Catholic Girls' Summer Camp called Schoenstatt and while playing with my best friend, I looked up and saw angels above the shrine. Immediately I felt an urge to go in and pray, this started my intimate prayer life with Christ.

When I was 14, I was at a Catholic teen event called Lifeline, and after the host was consecrated I looked up and saw the most beautiful eyes I had ever seen looking down at me from the Host. This image remained with me and I saw it a few more times that year. Later that year, I was reading the book *Heaven is For Real* and was intrigued when the boy kept talking about how beautiful Jesus' eyes were. For those of you who are not familiar with the story the boy, Colton, recognized Jesus' eyes in the painting that a young girl named Akiane Kramarik painted after seeing the face of Jesus. Out of curiosity I looked up the picture and was speechless to see that the eyes that I saw during Mass were undoubtedly the eyes of the painting. I had almost forgotten about seeing the eyes before seeing the picture.

In addition to these monumental miraculous moments in my life, from my childhood to early adolescence, God continued to shower His graces on me. I loved going to Mass and frequented confession. I was so blessed as a child to have such a real knowledge of God's love for me.

* * *

As I reached the end of middle school and started to prepare to go to high school I had an inkling that my faith would be challenged like it had never experienced before. This inkling presented itself in the form of the desire to get confirmed in 8th grade, which I was.

At the end of my freshman year of highschool I began to understand how childish my faith was. Not childlike as in trusting, but childish as in chasing the 'good feelings' of God. God was supplying the emotional highs sometimes known as spiritual consolation but I did not have a strong enough faith that could sustain itself between the "highs." At one point I was sitting in my brother's room praying and told God that I did not want to experience the emotional highs anymore. I needed a God that had more substance and I knew that I would not be able to find him in the high moments; I needed to find Him even if I couldn't "feel" Him.

The only thing I can say is God answers prayers.

For the next three and a half years of my life, I never experienced the emotional highs from God that were the basis of my childhood faith. At first I decided to supplement that emotional "proof" that God existed with intellectual "proof." Over the next several months I read excerpts from the Summa Theologica by Thomas Aquinas, some C.S. Lewis, and excerpts from the Catechism. I also talked to a priest about the doubts that I was beginning to experience. Through my research I was able to conclude that God existed, I just was not sure if He loved me.

During my sophomore and junior year of high school, my faith started moving to the backburner of my life. Intellectually I knew that God existed, but I had no relationship with Him, so I did not really care.

It was not until my junior year of highschool when I was brought face to face with the fact that I had no foundation in my life. The friends that I had based my life off of, were quickly spirling downhill and I was left trying to help them. At this point I had based off my meaning and my purpose in life on relationships. I knew, through my "research" that relationship was essential but I did not understand the difference between letting people use me and truly loving them.

I was grasping for some sort of foundation, so I turned back to my childhood foundation: my faith; only to find that God was seemingly not listening. I am not just talking about Him not answering an occasional prayer. I am talking about laying down in front of God and begging Him to return to my life. Challenging Him with the question, "Do you love me?" Yet, I heard nothing. I felt like an absolute fool for continuing to fall back to God because there was never an answer. I had been praying to a wall for three and a half years but I still could not find it in myself to give up on what I already did not believe in.

As a side note, I want to point out that throughout this entire time I was still attending Mass at least weekly, I was going to confession consistently, My habits never changed, my heart did.

* * *

During my senior year of highschool I started attempting to restart a prayer life and signed up to go on a Steubenville Conference that coming summer. I had heard so many good things about the conference; I figured it was time I finally went. Plus a friend invited me to go with her.

I entered into the conference filled with anger; filled with hurt; filled with humiliation. For the life of me, I could not figure out why I had not given up yet! God obviously was not doing anything for me, if He even existed. I spent the whole first day of the conference frustrated with the couple thousand overzealous Catholics. That night I was brought again into direct confrontation with the ultimate source of my frustration, the King of the Universe Himself. I cried that entire night during adoration, not because I was "feeling anything", at this point I still barely believed in God, much less that He loved me. They kept singing "your overwhelming, never ending reckless love" and I kept thinking, "if you loved me, where have you been the last three and a half years of my life? Why have I laid prostrate in front of You begging you to come back into my life and I never heard anything?!" The person next to me even was overcome with the spirit and I only grew more angry. I could not let God into my life, because I had been trying for years and the only response I ever got was, "...". My wall was built around my heart, I was done.

On Saturday I went and found a youth minister, whom I had gone to World Youth Day with and explained all of my frustrations. He patiently listened to me and at one point he asked me, "Well, why haven't you given up?" I had no idea. He proceeded to pull a bracelet out of his pocket and told me that he had bought this today without knowing why and who it was for but now it was evident that it was for me. The bracelet had the parable of the footprints on it and it read, "when you have seen only one set of footprints, my child, is when I carried you." He then challenged me to go into adoration with an open mind.

I want to take a moment to pause this story and invite you to look at the beginning. There is no logical reason I should be hating God right now, I had everything going for me. I had parents who gave me more real religious education before I entered high school than most people get in a lifetime. My childhood was one profound encounter after profound encounter of our Lord. Basically by the time I was 13, if I messed up anywhere in my life it was my fault. I was set up for success. So why, at 18 am I crying in adoration because I was so angry, I could not stand being in the same room as God? I do not know.

Regardless, I went back to adoration that night with somewhat of an attempt to have an open mind. Even though I had told God, "last chance" countless times, I cynically told Him last chance again. I went to confession right before adoration that night and ended up walking back halfway through the talk, "The Cross Revealed," by Brian Greenfield, just in time to hear something that ultimately changed my life. He said that "sometimes we are sitting in adoration surrounded by thousands of people on fire singing, 'your overwhelming never ending reckless love' and you are sitting there only believing part of that. You believe 90% of that kind of love but the 10% is questioning where God was when 'this' happened."

This immediately caught my attention because those were the exact words I had on my heart less than 24 hours before. He continued to explain that he did not know why God acts the way He does but he does know what God did for each and every one of us. Brian then proceeded to stretch out his arms in the shape of a cross. There has to be a reason.

During adoration that night, for the first time in years I was overcome by God and began to rest in His presence. During this time God showed me why I had not given up on Him. Throughout the last three years of my life, when I thought God was not listening to me or was just ignoring me, it was evident that His hand had always been in my life. Every time I almost gave up, He had put something or someone in my life to pull me back to Him. Even though my heart was too blind to understand it at the time, God continued to work through others to keep me close to Him. I could give you example after example but I do not think it is necessary. I realized in that moment that these less flashy reminders that God exists are equally as true and as good as the more flashy reminders of my childhood. God had spoiled me so much as a child I lost the ability to recognize Him in the ordinary. In addition to giving me an explanation of my past that night, God showed me my future. Not in a clear sense of what exactly my vocation is or what I supposed to major in, rather in a deep understanding that it would be good. There was a promise of good in the future.

* * *

That fall I started attending the University of Minnesota - Duluth and became more and more involved in the Newman Center on campus. God, working through Steubenville that summer, had planted a seed but the Newman Center gave me the practical way of living out my faith. God has kept His promise of a good future and has continued to shower His blessings on me constantly.

So I had my foundation built as a youth. I had my conversion as a young adult. I was missing one thing, but I did not realize it yet. One night, I was in my dorm and I was praying with some scripture that had been bugging me. The verses include: Matthew 12:36, Psalm 63:3, Matthew 12:33-37, Matthew 6:14, and Mark 9:41-50. The main theme of these verses is that there is no such thing as a half-hearted Christian. At the time I disagreed. I thought it was acceptable since, in every single other situation in life it was completely valid to be mediocre. I kept being confronted with the truth that you cannot be a half-hearted Christian. That night in my dorm I had a terrifying realization. If God exists and if His nature is love and if He actually sacrificed Himself for our salvation, then I had no chance of getting to heaven if I continued living the way that I was living.

I made the decision to give myself to God, because anything less is worth nothing. I would like to say I have been completely successful at that but that would be lying. However, the decision that I made that night to pray every day has fundamentally changed me. God has worked wonders in my life and I can truthfully say that I have a relationship with Him.

* * *

Every part of my life happened for a reason. Which is the most generic thing I have ever said, but hear me out. I can talk intellectually to people about God. I know my theology. I do not foolishly believe. I also understand that knowledge without a relationship is futile; I hated the God that I knew so much about because we did not have a relationship. I am so grateful for the people who listened to God pulling their hearts to remind me to not give up hope when I was too stubborn to realize what was right in front of me. God is good. God is love. That is His nature. He can be nothing but.

Ryan Myklebust

"I am the way and the truth and the life. No one comes to the Father except through me. If you know me, then you will also know my Father. From now on you do know him and have seen him."

-John 14:6-7

Growing up, my family went to church on Christmas and Easter but we did not acknowledge God any other time. My dad read a Children's Bible to me when I was young, but other than that I did not have exposure to church, the Bible, or Christ.

After high school, I attended a Catholic University. I chose the school for the strong sense of community. While I learned a great deal and made some incredible friends, I did not use this opportunity to develop my faith. I did take the two required spirituality classes. The first class was a Christian literature class. The syllabus stated that we needed a Bible of our favorite translation. I went to the bookstore and bought the cheapest Bible I could find. It happened to be the King James Version. Here is a quick excerpt from Romans:

"Or he that exhorteth, on exhortation: he that giveth, let him do it with simplicity; he that ruleth, with diligence; he that sheweth mercy, with cheerfulness." (Romans 12:8, King James)

I did not know who Jesus was. I did not know who Paul was, and I certainly did not understand how to read the King James translation. I struggled through the assignments and sat out of every discussion. I did not learn much about Christian literature in this class other than thinking that the Bible reminded me a lot of Shakespeare.

My next required religion class was Christian Spirituality. The grade was based on spending 30 minutes a day in quiet time journaling. The journaling prompts could be anything of our choosing. We were not encouraged or discouraged to journal about God. The assignments were simply to write about what we were feeling at that time. Needless to say, I did not have much faith formation during my undergraduate studies. If anything, my experience proved to me that religion is for people that need an imaginary friend or like the punishment of impossible-to-understand literature.

After college I accepted a job at a Fortune 500 company in the Twin Cities. I thought I could buy happiness. I had three cars, an ATV, a snowmobile, a dirt bike, a motorcycle and I had recently become a homeowner. I partied plenty and found time to make several trips to Vegas. I had so few commitments that in the fall of 2010, I hunted 17 out of the 18 possible hunting weekends. In addition to all my worldly possessions, I had a family that loved me and great friends.

I was passionate, but my attention span was short. Nothing I bought or did could keep my interest longer than a few months. I wanted more so, I started attending graduate school. My confidence was high. I had everything I ever wanted. I did not need a faith nor did I have time for God.

Even with all these activities to keep me focused, I managed to get distracted by a beautiful brunette named Melaine. There was something different about her. She had a confidence that I had never seen before. She was witty and put me in my place when my sarcasm crossed the line. Our first dates were about getting to know one another. Things were progressing slowly because Melaine was keeping her distance. By the fourth date Melaine did her best to get me to stop asking her out. We went to a nice restaurant and ordered a chocolate fondue. She looked up at me and said, "I am Catholic and everything that implies."

I thought about what she said as I chewed my chocolate fondue marshmallow. I responded with a profound, "Okay."

I had grown up with kids that went to Catechism on Wednesdays and, heck, I went to a Catholic University so I was pretty much Catholic! End of story. So I thought.

Melaine was disappointed in the lack of disgust in my response, so she continued. "Do you know what it means when I say I am Catholic? I go to church every Sunday."

"Oh" I said, as I thought to myself, "Church must suck when you are hungover"… insert fondue marshmallow.

She continued, "…and I am waiting until marriage."

Now she had my attention. Up until this point our conversations were fluff. We covered the topics you would talk about on a blind date. We chatted about where we were from, what our families were like, and where we went to college. But now things got serious quickly. When I say serious I mean our conversations turned serious, not our relationship. At that moment we stopped dating because I had no interest in living the lifestyle she was telling me she lived and she had no interest in living the lifestyle I was living.

There was that something different about her confidence that intrigued me enough to keep in touch. We became quite good friends. Many Friday nights, I would grab a 6-pack, a frozen pizza, and go over to her apartment with my list of questions about her lifestyle. We would play Monopoly and she would answer my questions. Her answers were consistent, well-articulated and thorough. She earned my respect and gave me a new appreciation for religious people. I was curious and began researching things like creation, God, and religion. I even began going to church every now and then with my sister.

At the same time I began thinking more about God, two events forced me to acknowledge that I did not know much about death. First, my maternal grandfather passed away. This was my first close relative to die. Prior to this, I had never needed to grieve or ponder what happens to a person after death. I knew the terms heaven and and hell but I did not know what it took to get to either place. I spent many hours wondering what happened to my grandpa Art.

The second event was meeting Melaine's family. Her mother had died suddenly five months before we met. Melaine had seven younger sisters so, I was expecting to enter a house filled with grieving crying girls who were lost due to the death of their mother. I was blown away by these girls. There was no crying, there were no crazy emotions, and there weren't any cat fights. They were getting along exceedingly well for having just lost their mother. On Saturday night, Melaine invited me to go to Mass with the family the following morning. I politely explained that I was not interested. But as I lay in bed thinking about the day, I wondered if the reason Melaine and her family were different was because of their faith.

The next morning, I attended Mass for the first time I can remember. I walked into St. Mary's Cathedral in St. Cloud and felt something. I could not explain it but I knew the reason Melaine was so confident and her family had been able to be strong so quickly after losing their mom was related to the feeling I got when I walked into the church.

A few weeks later, I was heading home from Monopoly with Melaine when I lost control of my vehicle. After swerving for several seconds, I came to a stop across the oncoming traffic. As soon as I stopped a semi-truck collided with my vehicle. The driver had done everything he could to avoid the collision but the ice made it impossible for him to maneuver around me. He was able to swerve enough to miss my driver side door which likely saved my life. The truck driver's quick maneuver caused the trailers; this was one of those two trailer rigs, to swing out. I braced myself for a second impact and this time my vehicle hit the axles between the two trailers. This prevented my vehicle from going under the trailer and potentially taking the top off my SUV. Both the driver of the truck and I walked away from the experience without injury.

I was relaxed during this entire experience. As my vehicle came to a stop across the highway, I looked over my left shoulder and saw the truck coming at me. I knew an impact was unavoidable. I was never scared. I never had a panicked feeling. I felt tremendously calm and I was 100% confident that I was going to be fine. I felt a peace in that split second that I had never felt before. I was uninjured by this accident but it changed my life forever. I spent the next five months of my life trying to figure out what that feeling was.

Up until this point, I had control of everything in my life. I did what I wanted, I went where I wanted, I bought what I wanted, I ate what I wanted and I got everything I ever tried to get. I was convinced that with enough effort nothing was out of reach. Seeing my grandfather pass and seeing Melaine's family without their mother made me feel vulnerable. It made me think that maybe I did not have as much control as I thought. Maybe I was just lucky. The accident put me over the edge. I woke up that next morning crying in my bed, because I had to acknowledge that I had been sitting across a highway in front of a semi and there was nothing I could do about it. I was humbled.

I realized that I was not in control. But just because I was not in control did not mean that God wasn't. I began to wonder, "Maybe God does care." I began feverishly researching God and His interactions with people. I started with interviews. I asked my friends why they believed in God. I called my friends' parents and asked them why they went to church. I invited my co-workers to lunch and asked them why they were Christians. I sat down with my sister and asked her why she got baptized. While every story had a different starting point, there were common themes. One of those common themes was Jesus.

I did not know who this Jesus man was, but I knew what I had to do. I had to read the Bible. I was so excited to find the New American Bible translation. If only I had known about it in college! I read the Gospel of John. Then I read Acts. Then I read Genesis and Exodus, then Matthew, Mark and Luke. I listened to podcasts, I read books and I researched on forums. I kept my job but I only did what I had to do to keep my boss from getting suspicious. I spent the rest of my days locked in offices reading about God. I continued to go to church. Some weekends I went to Saturday evening service with my sister and Sunday morning Mass with Melaine. Finally, I got to the point where the evidence was overwhelming. I had researched to the point where I could no longer deny God's existence or His plan for salvation. The biggest problem I had now was what to do about it. Do I really get baptized at 25 years old?

I kept my research project going to see if I could find a church that I felt comfortable joining. I attended several churches of different denominations. When I found a church I liked, I would look up their website and try to understand the foundations of that particular congregation. I was amazed to find so many similarities between the congregations I visited but equally surprised by the amount of focus on the differences. Several times I read why a congregation was splitting or why the pastors openly disagreed on topics. As a new "almost" Christian, the politics, positioning, and persuading made me uncomfortable. I wanted to join a church that was going to be around a while so I did not have to do this all over again when my pastor retires or moves. I began to appreciate the consistency of the Catholic Church. I had gone to numerous Catholic services, and by-and-large they were the same. There was a truth in the Catholic Church's consistency and history that created an aura authority that I could not find at other churches.

As my research continued, my questions became more complex and harder for Melaine to answer, so she introduced me to her friend Father Scott Pogatchnik. I prepared a list of questions not really knowing what to expect. I had never hung out with a priest before. We spent most of that first night getting to know one another and talking over John Chapter 6: the miracle of the True Presence of Jesus in the Eucharist. I was as impressed by Fr. Scott as I was by Melaine and her family. He seemed "normal." He was a great listener, he was not condescending, he was patient, and he had answers to all of my questions.

The next several weeks followed a version of this schedule. I would come up with a question from one of the Bible readings I had recently read. I would read about it in the Catechism, read other contextual Bible verses, I would ask Melaine, and I would email my family and ask them. If I did not get to an answer that I felt comfortable with I would discuss with Father Scott and he would help me understand and give me some verses to meditate on. I would then go over to Melaine's apartment and we would walk to the local Adoration chapel. Our conversations on the way to Adoration were filled with rebuttals like, "why", "it can't be," and "that does not make any sense." Our conversations on the way home were filled with comments like, "whoa", "did you realize" and "I cannot believe it is that simple." Much of the understanding I have about God's plan for salvation is from the connections I made while studying the Word in the Adoration chapel.

Even though Melaine and Father Scott had become my spiritual mentors I was still not convinced the Catholic Church was where I belonged. I became overwhelmed by the different church options so I tried to think like Jesus and the Apostles. If they were on the Earth today, where would they go to church? I came across the following letter from St. Justin Martyr:

> *"On the day we call the day of the sun, all who dwell in the city or country gather in the same place.*
> *The memoirs of the apostles and the writings of the prophets are read, as much as time permits.*
> *When the reader has finished, he who presides over those gathered admonishes and challenges them to imitate these beautiful things.*
> *Then we all rise together and offer prayers for ourselves . . .and for all others, wherever they may be, so that we may be found righteous by our life and actions, and faithful to the commandments, so as to obtain eternal salvation.*
> *When the prayers are concluded we exchange the kiss.*
> *Then someone brings bread and a cup of water and wine mixed together to him who presides over the brethren.*
> *He takes them and offers praise and glory to the Father of the universe, through the name of the Son and of the Holy Spirit and for a considerable time he gives thanks (in Greek: eucharistian) that we have been judged worthy of these gifts.*
> *When he has concluded the prayers and thanksgivings, all present give voice to an acclamation by saying: 'Amen.'*
> *When he who presides has given thanks and the people have responded, those whom we call deacons give to those present the eucharisted" bread, wine and water and take them to those who are absent."* CCC 1345

This letter was written a hundred odd years after Christ's death and it had a striking similarity to Catholic Mass. I realized that if I wanted to worship God the way the Apostles intended worship to be, I had to become Catholic.

Many things had to change: my views on sex and birth control, confessing sins to a priest, going to church every weekend, the belief in the mystery of the Eucharist, and on and on.I was not usually one to back down from a challenge, but becoming Catholic was different. This was going to be a lifelong commitment to a new lifestyle initiated by making an eternal covenant with the God that created the universe. The decision was not something I took lightly.

I struggled with making a commitment until May 22nd, 2011. On this particular Sunday, I attended a church I had not been to before with Melaine and her sister Kristin. They wanted to attend a church in Ham Lake, Minnesota. It was a beautiful sunny morning. The birds were chirping and the flowers had just started to bloom. We had chosen to sit in the exact middle of the church, directly under a large skylight. I was distracted during most of the Mass. I was trying to explain to God why I did not have to be Catholic. When it came time for Communion, I stayed in my pew and asked God if I should become baptized in the Catholic Church. All of a sudden, thunder boomed and many of the people in the church were startled. I looked up and saw the water running down the skylights directly above me and had a sudden and intense feeling of peace and calm wash over my body. I quickly recognized this feeling and immediately lost all control of my emotions. I started bawling like a baby. In that split second, God told me that He was with me now and He was always with me. I recognized that complete and utter calm as the same feeling I had right before I was struck by the semi. Even though I was not a believer in God's existence at the time, He was with me and He was protecting me.

An hour after Mass, my dad called me and told me that the readings from his church had reminded him of one of our recent conversations. It was unusual for my dad to call me to talk about faith. He had never done it before. I was standing in a Perkins waiting for a table so we did not discuss it much, but I know the Holy Spirit told my dad to call me that day to show me that there would be people around me supporting me in my decision no matter which church I decided to join.

After brunch I was bringing Melaine back to her car. We were saying our goodbyes and she looked over at me and said, "Ryan, I love you." I almost fell off the seat because she had told me only a short time earlier that she was only going to say that to her husband. I had not even told her yet what happened when she was up at

Communion, but she could tell something had changed in me that day.

I knew that day God was calling me to join His family as a baptized Catholic. I had experienced His love and I wanted to do everything in my power to make Him proud to have me as a son. On April 8th, 2012, at the age of 26, I was baptized, confirmed and received Him in the Eucharist for the first time. I had just finished the RCIA program at the Church of St. Paul in Ham Lake, MN. Four months later, Fr. Scott presided over the Mass at St. Mary's Cathedral in St. Cloud where Melaine and I celebrated the Sacrament of Matrimony.

My story does not end yet and my conversion continues every day. Being a husband and a father pushes me to need God even more than I did during my early twenties. I wrote this story to encourage those of you with questions about your faith or your church to make the time to go find the truth. It is out there. Jesus tells us, "Ask and it will be given to you; seek and you will find; knock and the door will be opened to you." (Matthew 7:7, New American Bible)

Lisa Cash

"...He who began a good work in you will bring it to completion..."

-Philippians 1:6

At the age of 46, I was the mother of nine living children. We started out with boy-girl twins who were then 22, then had two more girls, followed by five boys. I wished for another girl to help teach all these boys how to care for someone smaller than them, rather than just have another wrestling partner!

After our youngest son was born, we miscarried five babies (one set of twins). I so badly wanted life to have the last word. I tried many different things to become pregnant and stay pregnant. Diet changes, alternative medicine, different supplements. Less than 2 months from my 47th birthday – my husband, Rich, and I decided no more trying to conceive. A pregnancy and a new baby at our ages would be difficult and challenging. In a bit of a huff, I put the changing table at the curb with a "FREE" sign attached. We sold our 12 passenger van and bought a minivan that just fit us and our 6 kids still at home (3 in college at this time) and decided to accept being "done".

God has a sense of humor.

On November 30th, upon reading the Magnificat and seeing it was the feast of St. Andrew, I remembered I had prayed the novena to him the year before in hopes that we would become pregnant. Funny. Feeling a bit smug and disillusioned by my unanswered prayer, I decided to take a pregnancy test. I had no reason to take the test except to prove that the novena didn't work.

Imagine my surprise when the test came back positive.

Now I had a new reason to pray the St. Andrew novena – a healthy pregnancy and baby – due when I was 47 (and 8 months) old!

I wasn't sure how to break the news to Rich as I wasn't sure how he would feel about it after our recent decision to not get pregnant. I needn't have worried. Just as he had always been with previous pregnancies, he was thrilled that God had decided to use us to create another soul.

Having had so many miscarriages, it was natural for me to worry about the future of this little one inside me. But God is so good. About two weeks after discovering we were pregnant, I was laying in bed one morning when a bible verse came to mind. Now that is not something that usually happens to me as I have to admit I don't know many bible verses by heart. I heard the words:

He who began a good work in you will bring it to completion.

I knew I had heard those words before somewhere, perhaps a song? So I googled them and found out it was from the book of Philippians, chapter 1, verse 6.

I wrote in my journal that morning: *Laying in bed this morning, and this verse popped into my mind. I choose to believe God will sustain this baby and pregnancy.*

A week later I wrote: *He who began a good work in me will bring it to completion! Lord – help me to remember this verse whenever worry creeps into my thoughts about this baby and pregnancy. Please increase my faith.*

After having been disappointed by our previous miscarriages, we decided not to share our news with our children until we were further along. So while our family prayed the novena to St. Andrew that Advent, our kids were praying that we would have another baby, and my husband and I were praying that God would sustain this pregnancy and life would prevail.

At 9 weeks of pregnancy (1 week after I turned 47), we went to have an ultrasound. I was nervous. Ultrasounds this early in pregnancy had proven to be very disappointing and a source of grief. We were pleasantly surprised this time! In my journal I wrote: *Lord God, thank you so much! We had an ultrasound today. One baby with a very healthy heartbeat measuring right on at about 9 weeks! Such a relief and such a thrill to see that heart beating and see his/her little limbs moving all over. So beautiful! Thank you for this gift!*

All of our children happened to be home later that afternoon; the older three had not yet returned to college after their Christmas breaks. We gathered them all into the kitchen where we had a computer set up on the counter. Rich said he wanted to show them something. He clicked on the keyboard and the image of their brother or sister appeared.

Some of them were confused. What was that a picture of (at 9 weeks it is not real obvious, especially to a 6 or 9 year old who hadn't really seen that sort of black and white image before). We explained that we were pregnant and due in August. They were surprised, mostly in a good way. The older ones immediately began to worry, wondering if they would have to endure another devastating miscarriage and a mom who had to go through that again. Even the youngest was heard to say at times early in the pregnancy, "… if the baby doesn't die like the other ones."

We were excited, but also kept our guard up as the question of "What if?" was always in the backs of our minds.

A couple days later, we got the full report of the ultrasound. In addition to a healthy baby, the images had revealed some not so good news. I had sub-chorionic hematomas – some bleeding inside the womb. If the spots of bleeding continued to grow, a miscarriage could occur. I prayed the hematomas would shrink and go away.

I wish I could say that the bible verse I had heard while laying in bed a month earlier always kept me calm and trusting, but it didn't. I definitely had my moments of fear. For instance, I wrote a week later: *Lord, I realized this morning laying in bed that I am really scared. Scared about the baby. Scared that I will miscarry or have a stillborn or something horrible will be wrong with the baby. I'm scared I won't have what it takes to be a good mom to an infant. I'm scared the hematomas are growing instead of shrinking. I'm scared I'll start bleeding. I am just filled with so much fear this morning! UGH! Perfect love casts out fear, so Lord – please help me. I thought I was doing well with not worrying or thinking too much about things, but it's got me in its grip this morning. Deep breath. Lord, please increase my faith, hope, and love, and drive this fear out of me. Inhale light and exhale the darkness.*

A few weeks later, we had a level 2 ultrasound. I wrote beforehand, *Nervous yet excited to see our baby. May I be able to come home and tell everyone of the goodness of the Lord through the health of this baby.*

As part of my appointment, we met with a geneticist. This is a normal part of being pregnant at an older than normal age. We were offered some testing to see if the baby had any genetic issues. We decided to go ahead with the tests. The results would never change that I would do all I could to sustain its life, but If something was wrong or different with this baby, we wanted to be able to prepare our family and ourselves for that. We also wanted to put the minds of our moms at ease, who would understandably be worried about my and the baby's health when we told them we were expecting again.

Next came the ultrasound. The baby looked healthy and beautiful! The sub-chorionic hematomas had resolved themselves. Praise God! Oh, how I treasured seeing our little one moving around. Such a beautiful sight to behold! The devastating ultrasounds from the past four pregnancies did not have the last word; they only made me appreciate this life all the more.

We soon received the results from the testing. All looked good. And we were having a girl!

Not long after, I was reading the Magnificat in the morning as was my routine, and the meditation for the day seemed to speak directly to me. It read: "It is therefore in order to stimulate our desire that God delays its accomplishment, and so that, having obtained what we want, we may prize it higher, and preserve it with more solicitude and care." In response, I wrote: *This seems to be the case with me becoming pregnant now. I prayed for another baby for so long, and now that she's in me, I prize it all the more. It feels like a genuine miracle that God has chosen to bless us with.*

This little miracle continued to grow within me. However, it took a long time to be able to feel her kick. The ultrasound had revealed that the placenta was attached to the front of my womb, so it cushioned our little girl's movements. I tried to keep reminding myself that God would bring to completion the good work He had started in me, but I sometimes questioned if we had the same idea of what completion meant. I sure wanted the reassurance of feeling her movement!

One morning I wrote: *Lord, thank you for answering my prayers last night. I hadn't felt much baby movement and was starting to worry. I prayed a Memorare as I got ready for bed and then felt baby kicking last night and this morning as I lay in bed. What a joy! Thank you!*

At 20 weeks, I went in for another detailed ultrasound. Rich was there with me, as well as our 17-year old daughter, Sophie. The ultrasound tech moved quickly, explaining some things, but not giving us much time to process what we were seeing. It all looked good to us, and we breathed sighs of relief when the procedure was done and the tech left the room. However, within about 10 minutes, our relief would be replaced with fear. The perinatologist came into the room to explain what had been seen. Surprisingly, she asked me to get back onto the exam table as they needed to take another look at the baby's heart; the first images had looked like there might be a hole in it. The perinatologist now took hold of the ultrasound wand and zeroed in on the baby's heart. When the first images were not definitive, she added color to show blood flow. To her surprise, and our relief, that did no show any hole in our baby's heart. Tears of relief streamed forth from our eyes. Oh, thank you again God for good news!

From here on, the pregnancy continued fairly uneventfully. Because of my age, I had more frequent appointments and ultrasounds. The kids enjoyed being able to feel the baby kick and eventually watch and be in awe of the movements she made as my abdomen rolled like ocean waves. Our older daughters and I had fun buying baby girl clothes. I thoroughly enjoyed being pregnant and tried to imprint this experience in my mind one last time.

He who began a good work in me brought it to completion.

In the early morning hours of Saturday, August 4, 2018, our daughter was born. She gave us one last scare with the umbilical cord wrapped around her neck three times. Later that morning, most of her brothers and sisters came to visit at the hospital. It was the first of many times that they would take turns holding her and being amazed by her.

The next day we named our little girl Zelie Marie. Rich had prayed early in the pregnancy to Saint Thérèse of Liseux that this baby would survive and be healthy, so we decided to name her Zelie in honor of Saint Thérèse's mother. Her middle name is Marie for Mary, the Mother of God. What better way to honor the God by whose mercy life had the final word.

Heather Pfannenstein

"You made us for Yourself, O Lord, and our hearts are
restless until they rest in You."

-St. Augustine

I grew up in a loving family that has a dedicated and dynamic relationship with Jesus Christ. My dad is an Assembly of God Pastor and I was baptized and raised in the churches he pastored. My older brother and I were actively involved with the church ministry and music with my parents. It was our norm to go to church every Sunday morning, Sunday evening, and Wednesday evening. Through the example of their lives, my parents instilled a devotion and love for God that has always been deep in my heart. I am so thankful for my heritage. Because of my heritage, God has always kept my heart near to Him, even in the most difficult times.

In 2007, I was hired as a piano accompanist for the choir at Mary of the Immaculate Conception Church in Rockville, Minnesota. This was basically the first time I went to a Catholic Mass. I held that position for three years and played for them every Sunday morning. I also attended an Assembly of God church service every Sunday morning before I played for the Catholic Mass. Playing for the choir was a great experience full of wonderful men and women. It quickly became a highlight of my week.

In that time, I met Daniel, who was in the choir. We hit it off and began dating. Daniel was raised Catholic. He has a loving family that is very devout to God and the Catholic Church. After several years, our relationship was progressing and Daniel and I began talking marriage. We had always supported each other's own personal decisions of where we attended church and we really just ignored the most difficult conversation and questions: How do we combine our backgrounds? Does Daniel leave the Catholic Church and attend the Assembly of God church with me? Do I leave my church and attend the Catholic Church? Do we attend both churches? What about kids? Whose church are they baptized in? Are they raised in both? What about the different teachings in our churches? Which church is right? Which is wrong? All of a sudden, there seemed to be more differences than similarities.

Clearly, these were really important questions. Daniel and I only agreed on one thing: God was much too important to compromise. We didn't agree on any other answer to those questions, so we broke up. In our time apart and with no communication, Daniel and I were fervently praying for answers and drawing close to God in our own ways and in our own church communities. The truth is, my heart was hard and judgmental toward all things Catholic. I feared and diminished what I didn't understand. During this time, my dad challenged me to soften and open my heart and allow God to reveal Himself to me. What a challenge this was. I continued to battle this through prayer.

After several months, Daniel and I began talking again. Conversations reignited the spark we had. We decided to try to answer those questions and come to an agreement. Daniel decided to take a break from the Catholic Church and join me at my church. He did this all summer. By the end of the summer, Daniel was longing for more and was feeling empty. He told me he couldn't live without the Eucharist in the Holy Catholic Church. I still didn't understand this emptiness he described because of not receiving the Eucharist. Although I didn't understand, I was beginning to be able to respect how he felt. I was trying to open my heart, at least enough to respect Daniel and his convictions. But I didn't feel that way and I didn't want to give up my church. Everything felt like it was unraveling again.

After a Sunday morning at my Assembly of God Church, Daniel and I knew we had to make a decision and move forward, either apart or together, forever. For the first time in over a year, Daniel and I had a conversation about our churches without arguing and fighting. The Holy Spirit was truly present in our hearts, words, and conversation. It was very different than any conversation before. There was peace among us and in our hearts. I found a new profound peace that was unexplainable. I knew in my heart that Daniel was the man I should spend the rest of my life with and the Holy Spirit provided the peace to move forward with Daniel. For us, it was essential that we raise our kids in unity, even if our backgrounds were different. We made the decision that Daniel would stay Catholic and although I would never become Catholic, I would support him and raise our children in the Catholic Church. He agreed to support me when I wanted to go the Assembly of God church, even if that was weekly. Through the grace of God, we were unified in our decisions.

In the next couple months, we were engaged with a wedding date set for another year out. We continued to abide in God together through prayer, reading scripture, and challenging ourselves to grow in love and knowledge of God. Through abiding in Christ, His peace and Holy Spirit continued to prepare us for the Sacrament of Marriage. I joined Daniel in the St. Mary's Cathedral choir in St. Cloud. Even though I wasn't Catholic, I was very accepted and welcomed.

We were married November 8, 2014 at St. Mary's Cathedral. The ceremony was beautiful and incorporated our closest loved ones. It was important for us to honor both of our backgrounds as we officially began our life together. It was very special to have my dad as a co-celebrant in the ceremony. Our Gospel reading was Matthew 5:16, "Let your light shine before men, that they may see your good works and give glory to your Father who is in heaven." This was and is the mission for our marriage. Though our backgrounds were different, we knew God was the light in our lives and the unifying factor for us.

About a month after our wedding, during communion, God audibly spoke to me, for the first time in my life. He said, "Come to my table." I said, "No. I'm not ready." "Come to my table," He said a second time. I said, "No." again. He said it one more time, "Come to my table." I said, "Okay, I will, after our first child." Well, I thought I was being so very smart and buying time, because Daniel and I wanted to wait several years before having any children. I kept what God said to me to myself and didn't tell anyone, even Daniel. But, God's will always prevails. The next month, Daniel and I were unexpectedly pregnant. I was a bit terrified because this wasn't my timing. I also knew in my heart, that I had told God I would enter the Catholic Church after our first child.

The truth is, my heart was ready. God had been working on my heart since 2007 when I began playing piano in Rockville. God had been softening and preparing my heart for the Catholic Church that whole time. But my perspective was so limited and it wasn't until reflecting back on the journey that I could see how God was refining my heart for His will. My heart was ready, but I wasn't accepting

God's will because of the fear of facing my family and what they would think of me becoming Catholic.

Several months into our pregnancy, I finally told Daniel how God spoke to me. Daniel continued to support me, but he never once made me feel pressured to become Catholic. I had many questions about the Eucharist and Catholic Church. One of Daniel's strengths is his love to deepen his knowledge of God and the Catholic Church. As God tells us in his word, "As iron sharpens iron, one person sharpens another," Proverbs 27:17. My questions continued to ignite Daniel and the more he shared with me, the more we learned and grew together and the more God drew me to His table. I began to know that the mystery of the Eucharist was far more than I could explain. I knew the Eucharist was the presence of God in way I'd never known or experienced. Before Daniel and I were married, I felt resentment that communion was not open to other Christians who were not Catholic. But now, believing what the Eucharist was, my heart was healed of resentment. I learned to value how the Catholic Church kept the Eucharist so sacred. Daniel once asked me if I missed not receiving communion. I told him, yes of course I miss not receiving communion, but even though I can't receive it, I would rather be before the presence of God in the Eucharist, than anywhere else.

On October 5, 2015, we had a little boy named Matthias. His name means, "Gift from God." Matthias is our greatest joy and gift in the whole world. This gift of God would help fulfill God's will for my life. My heart was so full of joy, but it was also heavy and longing to "come to the table." Each Sunday my desire grew for the Eucharist. My heart and soul longed to receive Christ in the Eucharist. I knew I had to be obedient to God's calling and I knew it was so important for the future of our child as well.

Finally, in December of 2016, I told Daniel that I had to enter the church and do it soon. We met with Father Scott Pogatchnik and he led us through a plan so that I could enter the Church at the Easter Vigil in 2017. From the moment I decided to become Catholic, the longing for the Eucharist only grew. It actually become painful and filled me with sorrow not to receive the Eucharist. I knew that the Eucharist is the real presence of Christ, in a new and tangible way that

I had never experienced. I could feel His presence just by being around the host and in adoration, but I longed to taste and see His Presence. After ten years of attending Catholic churches, God had transformed my heart and lead me to enter fully into the Catholic Church.

My journey coming into the Church was beautiful. I was so blessed to have my husband, Daniel, by my side. He is a pillar of faith for me. I faced my fear of telling my parents and family about entering the Catholic Church, but when it's God's will, He goes before us and prepares the path. My parents and family did have some questions, but after talking it through with me, they were very supportive. Both sides of our family were with us as I entered the church at the Easter Vigil Service. God is so good!

I have never felt as if I am missing a spiritual aspect by being in the Catholic Church. I always feel God's presence in church and in the Eucharist. I feel and hear Him in the prayers, songs, and through the love of the church community. I know Jesus is the Bread of Life and transforms the Eucharist at every Mass, no matter what I feel. God is so real and so tangible. How important it is to be still and allow ourselves to abide in the Father, Son and Holy Spirit. The more I abide in Christ through prayer, devotion, Adoration, and through receiving the Eucharist, the more my soul is at peace and rest.

As Saint Augustine states, "You have made us for yourself, O Lord, and our hearts are restless until it rests in you."

Ben Owen-Block

"Now may the Lord of peace himself give you peace at all times and in every way."

-2 Thessalonians 3:16

I'm a senior in high school. I was raised Catholic, and my family is very involved in our church. I went to Catholic grade school and joined the children's choir for my church in the second grade. When I moved to the public school system for junior high, I joined the adult choir for church. Choir rehearsal was at the same time on Wednesday nights as religious education. I could not go to both, so to remedy this problem my mom took it upon herself to start a class that met on Sundays for the three of us kids and any of our friends. It was my brother and sister, their friends, a priest, some older kids as mentors, and then later me as well. When my siblings and their friends got confirmed, the Sunday class ended because there weren't enough people to keep doing it. So I continued to go to church choir rehearsal, and we called that good enough.

I won't lie; I was raised Catholic, but I didn't always enjoy going to Mass on Sundays. It was never a place of spiritual rest for me. Honestly, I went because I was in love with the music. I liked being part of a talented group of musicians; I felt valued and respected because I was in an adult choir. It felt that I belonged. Despite that music can be a good form of prayer, I only participated to sound pretty. In ninth grade, a friend invited me to audition for the National Catholic Youth Choir, based out of St. John's University. It's a week-long summer camp to rehearse choral music and tour the Midwest performing concerts. I auditioned, and was accepted. It was an amazing experience to sing so continuously and learn how music and faith intersect with one another. We sang a lot and got to talk to monks and experience their faith in an amazing way through music and prayer with them. I've been a part of this choir for four years now.

After my first summer with the choir, I was very excited to take Confirmation class my sophomore year to help me explore the different parts of my faith that I had numerous questions about. It was great to be back in a formal education setting for religion. The class helped me realize that Mass wasn't all about the music even though I had never particularly liked going to a Mass that had little or no music.

During my junior year, planning for a mission trip to Peru began, and I pounced on it as soon as I could. Something about it made me feel like I had to go. There was never a thought in my mind questioning if I was going. It was just assumed. I never asked why. Only after the trip did I realize how present God was in all these moments.

Summer came around, and I left for my week of singing with the National Catholic Youth Choir. It was a great week, and I really felt connected to my faith by the end of it. An hour after our final performance, I swapped suitcases and headed to the airport for Peru. On the way to Peru, I was super frustrated that I hadn't gotten any down time after the choir camp because I needed to rest and recharge. Thankfully, I slept quite a lot on the three plane rides to Peru, so I didn't get a chance to complain to anyone or brood on my own thoughts of self-pity. When we arrived, a group of full-time missionaries greeted us, and from that moment on I was happy. Throughout the whole trip, I never felt the need or even the urge to complain about anything. Those were the eight best days of my life up to that point. We did so many different things to help out the community that we were staying in, and our days were very full. Even though nothing was easy and there was plenty to complain about, I was completely content–for eight days straight.

One of the most impactful parts of the trip was the requirement that everyone gave testimony while they were there. I've always heard that everyone struggles with the same things and that no one is perfect, but it wasn't until I heard someone give testimony that it struck me how true it actually is. I heard many different testimonies, and it was beautiful to see how no one judged each other for their struggles and everyone supported each other in their awesome God moments. I was afraid to give my testimony because I didn't know what to say, but when the time came, I spoke, and it was a freeing experience. I didn't think I would have much to say, but I did. I was able to talk about where I was with my faith and why, though I had never done that before. It made me a lot more self-aware of my faith and brought forth new questions for me about my faith that I never realized had been there. It's hard to answer a question you didn't know you had. In all, the Peru trip made me more aware of my own faith–something entirely new to me.

Coming home from Peru, I again slept on every flight, but I was a different person. I was on top of the world! When we got home, we had to take a pill in case we had gotten parasites from the water. I didn't think that I had gotten any parasites while in Peru, but I took the pill anyway. A few people who went got sick because of the pill. This was normal. We were told that would happen if you did actually have parasites because they would fight the medicine. I, on the other hand, had a different kind of reaction. It was not a physical reaction, but rather an emotional one.

The day I took the pill (the day after we got back) happened to be the Fourth of July, and I went to the YMCA to go swimming with some of my cousins. The morning started out fantastic, but a few hours after I took the pill, I started to snap at people, and my day turned sour. It was really confusing because I had been on top of the world only a few hours before, and now I had no idea what was happening to me. My mom was very concerned for me due to my sudden mood change. We determined that it must have been because of the pill as that was the only thing that had happened since I had gotten back from Peru. What followed was the worst week of my life. I went to Adoration every day because I had decided at the end of the Peru trip that I was going to do it when I got home. I went to adoration right after I got back (before the pill) and it was awesome. I felt more connected to God in prayer than I ever had in my life. After taking the pill, I felt nothing at all. I went in and tried to pray, but I couldn't focus, I tried to journal and read scripture, but I couldn't manage to do it. It felt like the hardest thing in the world to do. I forced myself to go to adoration because I knew that it was the right thing to do and I had decided to in Peru, but I really didn't want to at all. I clung to the memory of how I felt during my time in Peru, but it was completely gone for me.

All week I had one awful day after the next; I would wake up feeling terrible, have a terrible day doing nothing, and go to bed feeling worse than the morning only to wake up the next day to feel no better than the night before. I lost all of my prayer life, I stopped smiling, and I honestly couldn't think of a reason to live. I tried and searched, but I couldn't find a reason. I knew that I had had reasons in the past, but I couldn't remember what they were. I cried so many times that week out of frustration and fear at what was happening to me. I was petrified because it felt like it would never end. My life was crumbling around me.

Thankfully, I have amazing family and friends. My mom was really concerned about me, so she contacted Tricia, who went to Peru with me, to have a Peru reunion to hopefully help me get better. The reunion was a cover to get me back around the people with whom I'd had such life-changing experiences with. We didn't tell them what I was going through because I didn't want it to change how they acted. I just wanted a party, and it was great! For two or three hours I was myself again, and I smiled for one of the first times all week. I was happy, but when I went home, all of that evaporated again. It was scary how fast it disappeared. There was an army of people praying for me by the end of that week: the missionaries who were still in Peru, my extended family, priests we knew, the entire church choir, some of the people who went to Peru with me, family friends.

One of the biggest fears I had was about the upcoming Steubenville trip which started at the end of that week. It was going to be my first time going to the conference, and I didn't know what to do because I was going to be in a massive room filled with people feeling the way I had a week earlier, while I was going through my own personal hell. Despite this, I was determined to go anyway.

The night before I left for the conference, I sat down to eat dinner with my parents, and my mom got me to smile just a little. She was persistent all week about trying to cheer me up, and she finally succeeded a little bit. As dinner continued, she got me to open up more, and I started talking more normally and smiling. I sang that night for the first time all week, which normally would've been happening because I love to sing, and it makes me happy. By the end of that night, I felt normal again. The next morning, I left for the trip and still felt like myself. I was back to being a normal human being, thank God!

The entire trip and conference was a huge blessing. Not only was it exactly what I needed after my awful week, but it was also exactly what I needed after my Peru trip. Peru was about the physical acts of God and living out His mercy, where the conference was about all of the other parts that I'd been missing so long. It seems every speaker was talking right to me. I know that their talks were geared for the audience and to feel written to each and every person, but they still felt like God was giving them right to me. One of my favorite quotations from the whole conference was "Run as fast as you can towards Heaven, and then look around to see who is keeping up. Make friends with them so you can push each other to run faster." It struck me because I had never thought about how urgently we need to seek to change our lives and center them on Jesus to help us get to heaven. That starts now, not later when we feel more pious.

On Saturday night of the retreat, instead of another speaker, we had three hours of Adoration. They brought out the monstrance and processed it around the entire convention center, but something made me unable to look at it, so I buried my face in my hands and prayed. As I was praying, the word "missionary" kept coming into my mind. At first I thought maybe I had imagined it since I had recently gone to Peru, but the more I tried to focus on praying instead of Peru, the more the word "missionary" came back. I realized that it wasn't from me at all but put there by God as something He wants with my life. I wrestled with it for a long time because I already had a loose plan for my life: go to college, get a job, and work for the rest of my life until I can retire. A little more complex than that, but you get the point. I eventually surrendered myself to God's will during that time of Adoration, and the moment I did, a wave of peace fell over me. My mind was absolutely clear for the first time in my life, and I burst into tears at the perfect peace and joy I felt. So I knelt there in my own private life changing moment with my face and a mess of tears in my hands as they processed the monstrance around.

After a little while, I felt a hand on my left shoulder to comfort me because I was crying, and then it shifted to an arm around my shoulders. The hand, however, on my shoulder had been different. I was more aware of it than I should've been, and it had been coming from the wrong angle. It had been as if someone was standing behind me and leaned over to put their hand on my shoulder, but I knew that everyone else was also kneeling. In some imperceptible way the hand felt very different from any other hand I'd ever felt. I could feel it on my skin even though I was wearing a t-shirt and a heavy sweatshirt.

I noticed all of this, but it didn't really mean much to me until after the trip, and I never told anyone about it. On the bus ride home, I shared my surrender because it was important to me. I never mentioned the hand on my shoulder however. When we were unloading the bus after the trip, one of the chaperones approached me and told me that she had to tell me something that might sound crazy even though we hadn't talked much in the past. She said that during Adoration she saw Jesus behind me laying His hand on my shoulder. She could tell I knew exactly what she was talking about. Everything made so much more sense to me as soon as she said that.

When I kneel down in prayer, I can still feel exactly where each one of Jesus' fingers touched me. Since then, I have been sharing my testimony as proof that God is still alive and working in this world, and I've been praying to figure out what sort of missionary God is calling me to be. I applied for a month long mission trip, but it fell through, so my current plan is to go to college in the fall and continue listening for what God wants me to be doing in my life. There are so many ways to be a missionary, and I know that I am going to be one, I just don't know what kind yet.

Sr. Anne Thérèse Wilder, O.P.

"Everything is Grace."

-St. Thérèse of Lisieux

Each moment of our lives is a gift, a moment of grace. With hearts attuned to the Holy Spirit and eyes accustomed to looking with faith, we can see how God is breaking through ordinary events to touch us with His grace and draw us to Himself. I witness this daily in my interactions with my students. Their innate faith and trust in God, their heartfelt prayers, and their joyful enthusiasm are a constant source of inspiration and a call to remember the blessings of God. They are also a reminder that the Kingdom of Heaven belongs to such as these. I count it one of the greatest blessings to be a part of their journey toward God and to participate in their education. It was never part of my plan to be a teacher, but I praise God for the graces He bestowed which directed me to my place of service in His kingdom.

The monotonous beep of the heart monitor. The knot in my stomach. The pale figure laying upon the bed. Wide-eyed, I stepped forward with trepidation. My mother leaned close, softly encouraging, "Don't be afraid. It's Grandpa; just talk to him." But what to say when fear steals all words? My twelve-year-old voice finally stammered, "It's me, Grandpa. I love you." Throughout the days which followed, we spent many hours in my grandfather's hospital room. Steadily, he began to recover and gain strength. I watched as the nurses bustled in and out checking vitals, administering medication, answering questions, encouraging my grandpa to stay hydrated, and doing each task with genuine kindness and care. I loved the nurses for this. As I continued to watch and grow in admiration, I quietly decided that I would be a nurse. Such was the nascent plan I conceived for my future.

Throughout high school, I continued to think about nursing school. I devoted myself to my AP Biology and Anatomy and Physiology classes. My mom, herself a nurse, was a steady source of inspiration and encouragement. Diligently, I researched nursing programs and contemplated college visits. Everything was falling into place and all the pieces seemed to fit together perfectly, perfectly according to my plan.

However, as this unfolded, I also began to feel the call to religious life. I felt drawn to belong totally to God, to live for Him alone. For a time, I discreetly researched religious communities online. The attraction to religious life increased. After connecting with Father Gregory Mastey, the Vocations Director of the diocese at that time, I found myself signed up for a four-day nun-run, a trip to visit various convents in a short amount of time. I had several misgivings regarding my decision to go no the trip, apprehensions which continued even into the first days of it. Why did I sign up? Was it a good idea to miss school? What was I thinking?!

Each of these reservations subsided when we arrived in Nashville at the motherhouse of the Dominican Sisters of St. Cecilia. As soon as I laid eyes on the convent, something in my heart stirred. In the evening, we joined the sisters for their night prayers. As the lights dimmed for the singing of the Salve Regina, my heart was filled with a deep peace, a peace I had previously never experienced. It was the peace of God's presence, and I felt I was at home.

The somewhat odd and startling thing about feeling myself called to the Nashville Dominicans was that they have a teaching apostolate. Teaching was certainly not part of any of my dreams for my future, but throughout my discernment I had fallen in love with the Lord. He had captured my heart. If He wanted me to be His bride in a congregation of teaching sisters, then that is what I would do. While this was my approach to my vocation, I can't say that nursing completely left my mind. There was a small lingering hope that perhaps I would somehow still become a nurse. I couldn't imagine my heart finding joy in any other way.

Almost two years later, in October of my senior year of high school, I accompanied other young women on a quick one-day in-state nun-run. I signed up to go, not because I was particularly interested in any of the communities we were going to visit—my heart was set on becoming a Nashville Dominican—but I wanted to support the other young women going on the trip. I did not have any particular goal for the trip or foresee any further development regarding my own vocation. I did not remember that the Lord is full of surprises.

One of the communities we visited was the Sister of Charity, a teaching order. After our time of refreshments and conversation, the sisters took us to visit their classrooms. We walked into one of the elementary classrooms and I was taken aback. As I peered around the room, the same peace I experienced in the chapel in Nashville again overflowed in my heart. I had the sense of God saying to me, "This is what I want for you."

Following our visit with the Sisters of Charity, we visited the Little Sisters of the Poor. As one of the sisters spoke about their life and shared a PowerPoint of pictures, I thought to myself, "This *should* be perfect. They're sisters, and they're nurses." Yet, as beautiful and joyful as these sisters were, I did not have the sense of peace or of homecoming that had been present in Nashville with the Dominican Sisters.

For some days following the nun-run, I pondered the events. What unexpected graces and confirmation from the Lord! I kept asking myself, "My—a teacher? Can I really let go of my dream of nursing?" But when I considered the peace I had felt walking into that classroom, my doubts dissipated. The Lord was showing the way, bestowing His grace, and I simply needed to trust and to follow.

After entering the Dominican Sisters of Saint Cecilia and professing my first vows, I began my education studies. Throughout my college courses, I knew I was where the Lord wanted me, but doubts resurfaced about whether teaching would suit me. I loved the Lord and so I would follow His will, but could I love teaching?

Student teaching followed at the end of my course work. I began my first placement in a first-grade classroom. The first lesion I taught on my own was a math lesson. Butterflies filled my stomach as I began the lesson, but as I taught it was as if something inside of me jolted and came alive. It was another confirmation for me that the Lord knew what He was about in calling me to a community with a teaching apostolate.

Throughout the past four years, I have grown in my love for teaching. I have noticed that the more I trust the Lord's plan, the more deeply Christ's peace is rooted in my heart. It is then that I notice the joy in guiding the children in their relationship with Jesus, in preparing them for the Sacraments, in helping the struggling reader, or guiding the student learning English. Each day is replete with graces, with the presence of God, and the children are my living reminder of that. A few months back one of my students stopped, looked up earnestly at me and asked, "Do you like teaching?" The question caught me a little off-guard as it seemed unrelated to our task at hand. But it was really a grace; God was inviting me to ponder again His mysterious yet loving plan which has filled my heart with joy and peace. "Yes," I replied, "I like it very much." And I wouldn't dream of changing it.

Colette Jemming

"When I am afraid, I put my trust in you."

-Psalm 56:3

Most of us have had the experience of falling in love or having a relationship with someone. Growing up in a Catholic family, I knew I loved God, but it didn't occur to me that I could fall in love and form a real relationship with Him. I always thought the relationship would be one-sided, but how mistaken and untrue that turned out to be.

Attending church every Sunday was a formed habit; I say "attending" because I was physically there, but my mind wandered as I blanked out during the homily and watched people walk past after communion.

Everyone has their own insecurities. It's a part of what makes every human perfectly imperfect. I'll just lay it out: I didn't love myself for who I was. Comparison was high on the list of what I spent my time doing every day. I couldn't seem to break the habit of looking at everyone around me and thinking, "Wow she's prettier than me, skinnier than me, has more friends than me...". Negative thoughts consumed my mind on a day-to-day basis as I closed myself off from almost everyone in my life. I thought that, somehow, if I was tough and showed no emotion, then everything would be easier. In my eyes, tears were a weakness. Hugging was uncomfortable. Showing any emotion was unacceptable.

The summer of 2018 rolled around, and my mom told me that she had signed my little brother and me up to go to a Steubenville Conference with St. Mary's Cathedral. I couldn't have been more upset. I fussed and complained that I wouldn't know anyone and hated being in situations where I had to talk to a lot of people. The day arrived when we packed our luggage and got onto the bus. I sat in the back, outermost corner of the bus. This was the farthest away I could get from any human interaction.

The weeks before this conference were probably some of the toughest I have ever experienced. It felt like I had built an indestructible wall around myself and hardened it so no one could see the pain inside of me. I felt so alone, even when surrounded by people. Surely no one could be experiencing what I was. These aren't easy words to read, even for myself, but it's the down-to-earth reality of what I was feeling at the time. There was an obvious conflict going on inside of me, not knowing if I should open up to others around me. I guess I was so afraid that no one would accept me for who I really was.

Back to Steubenville. After sitting on the bus, I immediately started realizing how different these youth were compared to the people I surrounded myself with. They seemed authentic and genuinely happy. Jealousy took a grip: "Why do they get to be happy.. and not me?" Attempting to push those thoughts aside, I tore down my wall just a little bit, thinking that, maybe, just maybe, if I open myself up a little bit, then I might be able to make a few friends on this trip. A small talk conversation quickly turned into laughter and playing games. These people were so easy to be around! The days went on and it was incredible how people wanted to be friends with the real me. Not someone that has the same opinions as them, agreeing with whatever they say, but the real me. This can be difficult sometimes, since I am a people pleaser. What this means is that in every group situation, I will try my hardest to make sure everyone else is having fun, that I say exactly what they want to hear. I didn't really know who I was because I was trying so hard to be like everyone else.

I was so tired of being closed off and hiding all of my insecurities. There was a point right before Saturday Adoration that a speaker asked the crowd members to stand up if they were truly ready to accept Jesus fully into their hearts for the first time. After deeply contemplating if I was ready to be that vulnerable, I stood up. The wave of relief that washed over me was something I've never felt before. I started crying. At that moment, I realized I was enough in God's eyes.

Also at this time before Adoration, I was talking with a friend that I really started to grow closer with. We were talking about crying, and I told him how I never cry. He opened up to me and started talking about how emotion shows the heart and how tears are beautiful. I had never thought about crying that way and it really impacted me.

Going into this trip, I wasn't very strong in my faith. Like I mentioned earlier, I went to Mass every Sunday, but that was about it. I knew some prayers, a few Saint names, and a few stories from the Bible. For those of you who have not been to a Steubenville conference, Saturday night is one of the most influential events of the trip.

I was kneeling down and praying to God. There was a point in Adoration when I opened up my hands and cried out in my head, repeating, "Jesus I give everything to you. I give you my sins, my suffering, my shame, all my vulnerabilities." Next thing I knew, my head was hitting the ground. Later, it was explained to me that I rested in the Spirit, but at the time I had no idea what was happening. The thing is, I've never felt such overwhelming peace in my entire life. I laid on the ground with complete surrender to God and with no control of my body. I couldn't hear or see anything. I tried so hard to push myself up and get back into my chair, because to be honest, I was scared and terrified to not be in control of my body, and a little embarrassed, but God was in control. Eventually I gave up trying, and just laid on the ground sobbing. I didn't have to depend on myself anymore or the people around me. I could place my trust and life in the hands of someone who was never wrong, who knew me more than I knew myself. Who would continue on loving me no matter how many mistakes I made. The overwhelming love of God consumed my heart. I wanted nothing more than to be with Jesus. I felt Jesus' presence there with me, and as my eyes were closed, I felt Him walk away. At this point my senses came back and I saw the priest walking away with the monstrance as Adoration came to a close. A few of the chaperones helped me into my seat and as everyone ran up to dance to the last couple of songs, I sat in my chair with my hands open on my lap. I felt a peace I never thought was humanly possible.

After Adoration I started laughing uncontrollably. The chaperones told me it was also a gift from the Holy Spirit. It felt like all of my troubles were no longer important, that my soul was so light and filled with life that it was almost like a sliver of what Heaven might feel like. My soul was so joyous that I continued on laughing for around two hours after getting helped back to my room.

I'll just leave it at this: the very good sometimes comes with the very bad. Sunday night around 3am I experienced major spiritual warfare. The devil did not want me to be loving God and sharing His love with others. To be honest, I had never been so afraid in my life. I had a very hard time accepting what I saw and felt my mind telling me that I was making it up. My 17-year-old mind was trying to convince myself that I was making up what I was seeing for attention, but a family friend affirmed that what I experienced was indeed true spiritual warfare. After the retreat was over, the mom of one of the girls that was bunking right next to me told my mom that at 3am on Sunday night she woke up and felt that her daughter was in danger and started praying the rosary, a powerful weapon against all evil.

Everything happens for a reason. If I would not have grown closer to God and strengthened my Catholic faith, I would never have been strong enough for what was to come.

Little back-story. I was a runner in High School. The sports package, cross country, Nordic skiing, and track. I trained so hard because I was captain, and as it was my senior year, I was more than ready to take my girls to state. As it turns out, God's plan was different than my own. My hip started hurting at the beginning of the season, not too long after getting back from the Steubenville retreat. Days turned into weeks and nothing was helping, not trips to the chiropractor, exercises, or taking time off from running. The strange part was that the X-rays did not show anything out of the ordinary. It got to the point where my normal stride had transformed into an obvious limp. I'm not one to complain, so on Halloween when I finally told my parents about the pain in my leg and hip that was hindering my ability to walk, we decided to get an MRI done. Already, I knew something was up because after going through with the scan, they did another one, then injected a contrast into my body to get a better picture, and did yet another scan.

The next day, I came home from school to find my mom crying and my dad home early from work. They sat me down and I already knew before they told me. I asked my dad more as a statement than a question, "It's a tumor isn't it". He broke down in tears and kept repeating, "I wish it were me instead of you." I have never seen my dad cry before, so this terrified me and hurt my heart. Sitting in shock, we drove to the doctor's office to see the scan. There was a bone tumor a little bit bigger than an egg that was wrapped around my S1 nerve within my sacrum.

I didn't know what to do. The doctors were unsure if the tumor was malignant because of how fast it was growing. I didn't know how to tell my friends, my teammates, or how I was going to be able to keep on functioning.

I had to wait a month, until December 3rd, to have the surgery. A month of not knowing if I have cancer or not. A month of trying to get through each school day. A month of trying to support my cross country team from the sidelines. I know that if I would not have created a closer relationship with God on the Steubenville conference, then I would've tried to rely on my own strength to keep me going. By relying on God and placing my life into His hands, I was able to stay strong through this turn of events.

At some point in their lives, everyone experiences what it's like to be at rock bottom. To be honest, I didn't have a lot of good friends, and the ones I had, I had grown apart from over the summer. Exercising is how I released most of my anxiety, and I wasn't able to do that anymore, so I started slipping back into a depressive state of mind. Now I had this bone tumor, something which I was completely terrified about, but had to be strong because the people who loved me needed me to be.

I received the sacrament of the Anointing of the Sick. According to Catholic doctrine, this sacrament serves as a channel for special graces from God that comfort and heal, physically and/or spiritually, people who are seriously ill and in danger of death. Something I never thought I would be doing until I was at least 5 times my current age. I felt relieved to feel such peace.

The surgery ended up being very successful. The doctors removed the tumor, which ended up being benign, and I started my recovery. I was on the third floor of the recovery area, in a children's section. Here I was, healing fine and feeling relieved, but I was so sad because all of these children around me were going through their own hardships. Some might've had cancer, others some sort of organ failure. The thing was, no matter their situation, these little kids were still so happy. I saw them smiling or just showing me that everything was fine. That's when I decided that no matter what life threw at me, I was going to keep smiling. I would spread joy to others and be happy because happiness is contagious.

Throughout everything I have been through I have learned that prayer is so powerful. I can place my trust and life in the hands of someone who was never wrong, who knew me more than I have ever known myself. It didn't occur to me that I could fall in love and form a real relationship with God. He has given me the strength to not be afraid. He has given me the strength to open myself up and accept whatever comes my way while depending on His courage and strength, and not my own.

Don't miss out on the first book of the series!